CBT as an Integrative Psychotherapy

CBT as an Integrative Psychotherapy explores the current key themes, approaches, and interventions in psychotherapy. Developed and based on a dialogue between trainee psychotherapists, colleagues, collaborators, and scholars, this book integrates theoretical and technical aspects of psychological interventions. Chapters link theory and practice and provide philosophical insights in an accessible and discursive manner. The authors conduct a thoughtful analysis of psychotherapy and cover several topics including conflict, acceptance, self-esteem, and pseudo psychology.

This book is discursive in nature and essential reading for novice and more experienced therapists. The integrative approach used throughout will allow trainees and practitioners to discover a coherent theoretical and practical framework for helping a diverse range of clients.

Clara Calia PhD is a clinical psychologist and senior lecturer in clinical psychology at the University of Edinburgh, UK.

Gian Luigi Dell'Erba is a clinical psychologist and a lecturer in the Clinical Doctorate in Italy.

Ernesto Nuzzo is a clinical psychologist and lecturer in the Clinical Doctorate in Italy.

Donatella Tamborrini is a senior psychotherapist and supervisor and a former visiting lecturer at the University of Edinburgh, UK.

"This book, authored by expert clinicians and teachers of psychotherapy in Italy and the UK, provides the theoretical basis and description of Integrative Psychotherapy. The treatment is distinguished from the other eclectic and pluralistic approaches, as it is based on a robust cognitive psychotherapy model. The book will be invaluable both for trainee and experienced clinicians who wish to learn an innovative psychological treatment with an original cross-cultural perspective"

Riccardo Dalle Grave, *MD, Director of the Department of Eating and Weight Disorders, Villa Garda Hospital Italy; Editor of the official Enhanced Cognitive Behaviour Therapy (CBT-E) website*

"The authors provide an important contribution to the field of integrative psychotherapy as well as drawing inspiration from philosophies such as Stoicism. Their integrative approach will allow students and experienced practitioners alike to discover a coherent theoretical and practical framework for helping a diverse range of clients"

Donald Robertson, author of *The Philosophy of Cognitive-Behavioural Therapy* and *How to Think Like a Roman Emperor*

"This text stems from the fruitful collaboration among psychotherapists and researchers and offers relevant insights to both trainee and experienced psychotherapists. Their aim is to illustrate some of the most meaningful aspects of cognitive-behavioural therapy in an integrated perspective."

Francesco Mancini, *Director of the Clinical Doctorate APC (Rome, Verona, Lecce) & Lecturer in Clinical Psychology*

"*CBT as an Integrative Psychotherapy* is a resource born from the collaborative dialogue between colleagues, students and researchers. The authors aim to integrate different aspects of psychotherapeutic interventions in a deliberately colloquial and accessible way, and to provide an integrated perspective of multiple aspects of Cognitive Behavioral Therapy (CBT) with several other psychotherapeutic evidence-based treatments"

Emanuele Rossi, *PhD, Scuole di Specializzazione in Psicoterapia Cognitiva, Società Italiana di Terapia Comportamentale e Cognitiva*

CBT as an Integrative Psychotherapy

Clara Calia, Gian Luigi Dell'Erba,
Ernesto Nuzzo, and
Donatella Tamborrini

Routledge
Taylor & Francis Group

NEW YORK AND LONDON

Cover image: ©Getty Images

First published in English 2024
by Routledge
605 Third Avenue, New York, NY 10158

and by Routledge
4 Park Square, Milton Park, Abingdon, Oxon, OX14 4RN

Routledge is an imprint of the Taylor & Francis Group, an informa business

© 2024 Clara Calia, Gian Luigi Dell'Erba, Ernesto Nuzzo and
Donatella Tamborrini

Translated by Donatella Tamborrini

Published in Italian by ALDENIA EDIZIONI SRL, 2021

Library of Congress Cataloging-in-Publication Data
Names: Calia, Clara, author.
Title: Cognitive behavioural therapy as an integrative psychotherapy /
Clara Calia, Gian Luigi Dell'Erba, Ernesto Nuzzo, Donatella Tamborrini.
Description: New York, NY : Routledge, 2023. | Includes bibliographical
references and index.
Identifiers: LCCN 2022060399 (print) | LCCN 2022060400 (ebook) |
ISBN 9781032289380 (hbk) | ISBN 9781032278858 (pbk) |
ISBN 9781003299226 (ebk)
Subjects: LCSH: Cognitive therapy. | Eclectic psychotherapy.
Classification: LCC RC489.C63 C35 2023 (print) |
LCC RC489.C63 (ebook) | DDC 616.89/1425--dc23/eng/20230414
LC record available at https://lccn.loc.gov/2022060399
LC ebook record available at https://lccn.loc.gov/2022060400

ISBN: 978-1-032-28938-0 (hbk)
ISBN: 978-1-032-27885-8 (pbk)
ISBN: 978-1-003-29922-6 (ebk)

DOI: 10.4324/9781003299226

Typeset in Times NR MT Pro
by KnowledgeWorks Global Ltd.

Contents

Preface

This is an innovative psychotherapy book, developed and based on a collaborative dialogue between trainee psychotherapists, international students, colleagues, researchers, and scholars. We are clinical psychologists, experienced psychotherapists, and researchers; our heartfelt purpose is to summarise meaningful aspects of psychotherapy and inform clinical practice, research, and teaching.

Underpinning themes of this book have been gathered from cognitive psychotherapy classes, dialogues with colleagues, supervision, and training workshops.

The requirement to reflect "on paper" about the content of such dialogues posed a series of practical challenges related to how a project can be translated into fruitful outcomes. Some challenges have been dealt with, some just attempted. As everything else, this effort can be improved, and as everything else it has limitations. The book originated from an Italian edition called "Notes on psychotherapy" (published in 2021), translated by Donatella Tamborrini and adapted by the authors for an international audience. This book includes various original materials like case examples and in-depth reflections on CBT from different cultural, clinical, and teaching environments.

The aim of this book is to integrate theoretical and technical aspects of standard procedures of psychotherapeutic interventions, along with theoretical constructs and specific aspects of general and clinical psychology and psychotherapy.

This work is intended for colleagues, particularly our early career colleagues. However, due to the complexity of certain themes, and to the technical and psychological and psychotherapeutic knowledge required to comprehend certain aspects of psychotherapy, we hope that experienced psychotherapist colleagues will also appreciate the several challenges posed by this book. This book links theory and practice, providing philosophical insights with discursive style that are missing in most clinical books on psychotherapy. The combination of such perspectives offers a comprehensive and integrative content for novice therapists and more experienced ones alike.

The keen reader will be able to delve into the matters explored in this book through the technical and theoretical passages through cross-references, notes, and recommended bibliography.

The text is deliberately colloquial, and the language is discursive in nature. This is because discourse is a crucial tool to reflect, analyse, and divulge complex concepts in an accessible manner. Philosophical discourses have reached us with their multifaceted and diverse presence, characterised by contributions, in the form of interviews or reflective dialogues.

Discourse empowers reflection, proactive dynamic knowledge, and learning. The aim is to offer a contribution towards the development of effective integrative psychotherapy, an approach characterised by uniformity, which may also respond flexibly to different aspects of human suffering. We believe that Cognitive Behavioural Therapy – CBT – offers significant contributions in this context.

Furthermore, key aspects of Integrative Psychotherapy are explored through discourse; a spontaneous, yet effective means to reflect, analyse, and divulge complex issues, with immediate clarity and conciseness.

The pervading aspiration of this book, however, consists in promoting an integrative contemporary and comprehensive cognitive perspective, which at its core leads to a conceptualisation of individuals' suffering and related behaviours' choices and solutions. These aspects are linked to individuals' ability to be self-aware and to understand themselves and others through behaviours and mental states. Furthermore, considerations on theory of mind and focus on function of individual behaviours and cognitions are a key aspect of this book.

Acknowledgements

A special thanks to Professor Corinne Reid and Dr Cristobal Guerra who provided precious and insightful feedback to the first draft of the book. Their experience as clinicians and researchers from different continents, Corinne works in Australia and Cristobal in Chile, stimulated inspiring discussions of the state of the art of CBT.

Introduction

Introduction

The purpose of the book is to offer a text based on a Cognitive Psychotherapy model, anchored on CBT model therapeutic fidelity, and provide examples of Integrative Psychotherapy, rather than just leaning on eclectic or pluralistic approaches. We aim to achieve this purpose by:

- Creating a dialogue between the four authors, a multifaceted lived experience, which affords potential to respond to complex presentations
- Modelling dialogue examples in clinical practice, to illustrate how clinical challenges can be approached through different perspectives. We will also discuss why complex presentations benefit from an integrative approach through case examples at the end of each chapter

As outlined by authors such as Norcross and Goldfried (2019), the attempt to integrate psychotherapeutic visions and interventions of different theoretical orientation has resulted in approaches such as:

- Technical eclecticism
- Structural integration
- Focus on common denominators
- Assimilative integration

Technical eclecticism is characterised by therapeutic interventions considered effective by psychotherapists, despite differences of opinion with its theoretical foundations. For instance, a psychodynamic psychotherapist may encourage in vivo exposure, when working with a patient who suffers from an anxiety disorder.

Structural theoretical integration is characterised by an innovative orientation, which aims to re-conceptualise constructs, techniques, and processes harmoniously to include, by redefining them, approaches that are considered valid.

DOI: 10.4324/9781003299226-1

Focus based on common denominators takes into consideration techniques and processes that are in superposition between different approaches, whilst bypassing typical features of such approaches. This is based on the understanding that common processes and interventions are those more robust as the foundation of evidence-based outcomes.

An assimilative integration approach is characterised by the attempt to re-conceptualise constructs, processes, and techniques, in the light of one approach that is considered promising and comprehensive in structure (Norcross & Goldfried, 2019).

We opted for an assimilative integration approach based on CBT (Norcross & Goldfried, 2019) throughout our work.

Although an assimilative integration approach may be disapproved of, as it is still incomplete and requires to be tested and validated on extensive population samples and by clinicians, it has the advantage to be utilised extensively, to be understandable and shareable with therapists trained in other approaches.

Cognitive Behavioural Psychotherapy is one of the most recognised and effective psychotherapies in the vast field of psychotherapy; it has historical ties with other kinds of psychotherapies and psychological treatments. CBT's clarity and specificity positions it as a gold standard, a point of reference for other psychological treatments, and a common ground for dialogue amongst psychotherapists belonging to different orientations.

Longstanding evidence suggests that CBT is the most beneficial psychotherapeutic treatment compared to others, for most mental health disorders (Dobson & Dobson, 2018).

CBT's development, its influences, and contributions in the psychotherapeutic field through the years and its several components make its widespread use valid and reliable. These are only a few aspects that have contributed to CBT's development and growth, as focus of clinical research and trials.

This work also aims to delve into specific aspects of Functional Analysis, also known as ABC, a common feature of several CBT approaches.

The system of hypotheses and premises on which several CBT applications are based is widely supported by research, and it is utilised in non-clinical settings, such as organisational psychology, educational and sports psychology, and couple psychology.

The wide range of cognitive and behavioural techniques is the result of the integration of an invaluable wealth of effective clinical interventions, which have been consistently substantiated over the years. A particular emphasis will be given to the therapeutic relationship, which sits above and across the use of techniques and is considered a primary component of therapeutic processes, in conjunction with the application of psychotherapeutic interventions.

As mentioned above, CBT is considered the most effective psychological treatment for psychological and psychiatric disorders; in certain instances, it is as effective as alternative standard treatments, such as pharmacological treatments (David, Cristea, & Hofman, 2018; Sturmey & Hersen, 2012). CBT is an effective additional treatment in the management of disorders whose primary aetiology is organic in nature, such as schizophrenia and bipolar disorder, just to mention current examples. This is because CBT not only addresses symptoms but also focuses on relapse prevention, and how to maintain its therapeutic benefits when treating such significant mental health illnesses.

One source of evidence in support of its effectiveness comes from the International Guidelines; CBT is always cited and included for the treatment of major mental health disorders (American Psychological Association, 2016; Emmelkamp et al., 2014; Huhn et al., 2014; Kazdin, 2008; Sakaluk, Williams, Kilshaw, & Rhyner, 2019).

Psychotherapeutic treatment according to CBT comes from its own complex historical evolution; however, it is also robustly anchored to real-life situations. Furthermore, CBT's development thoroughly reflects progress in knowledge of brain and mind development, with regard to normal and psychopathological processes.

CBT has always kept itself abreast of scientific discoveries concerning biology, psychology, brain functioning, behaviour, human relationships, personality, and well-being.

Thus, CBT is intrinsically integrative and empirical in its origin and purpose.

Integrative Origins

CBT stems from several epistemological and technical perspectives, which converge on an unambiguous stance towards its main focuses of interest: mind and behaviour.

We will focus on two main perspectives: CBT stemming from research and CBT stemming from clinical treatments.

CBT stemming from research

We may sketch the background of CBT against a remarkably cogent shift in the understanding of the mind, and related research on the features of functioning and behaviour. Such change in perspective, also known as the Cognitive Revolution, started halfway during the Forties and continued throughout the Fifties (Gardner, 1985a).

The critique which led to the cognitive revolution was based on questioning the general validity of learning paradigms such as the Learning Theories of Thorndike and Pavlov and Skinner's Operant Conditioning, which at that time were considered the only reliable scientific answer on learning and behaviour acquisition (Dobson & Dobson, 2018; Legrenzi, 2019).

Prior to the Cognitive Revolution and considerations regarding generic notion of information, psychology adopted a behaviourist paradigm to conceptualise behaviours (Legrenzi, 2019).

Behavioural acquisition might have been explained with causal association of certain behaviours with others, or with the fact that causal behaviours might have been successful.

Instead, explanation of behaviour throughout time was conceived through the idea that successful attempts, within a certain behaviour, would increase the likelihood of its occurrence, as well as unsuccessful attempts were characterised by intensely negative consequences such as pain or punishment, which would decrease the likelihood of such behaviours (Legrenzi, 2019).

Such findings, which derived from experimental studies, are valid for straightforward occurrences, such as dog training, or certain actions in infancy. What has radically changed is that we all need goals and objectives as human beings, which we desire and are motivated to pursue, and in doing so we create expectations, convictions, or beliefs that simplify our plans.

This knowledge aimed at achieving goals is limited and requires consideration of experimental psychology and objectives of clinical psychology.

A further shift in perspective, also known as Communication Theory, emerged from a formal, mathematical perspective developed by Claude Shannon and Norbert Wiener (Legrenzi, 2019) and embodied the theoretical platform from which advanced computer technologies, or promising applications, such as language processing, were developed.

A key turning point linked to the development of Communication Theory is the typology of the technologies developed; in fact, computers, albeit simplified and formalised in their functioning, were the testing ground for Human Information Processing, also known as HIP paradigm. This reflects a shift in focus from studying events and related behaviours, i.e. targets of behaviourist psychology, to mental processes.

Gradual change of the panorama, once a cognitivist breakthrough had taken place (i.e., that our actions are influenced by what we think, not just in response to some external stimulus-response learning), was characterised by a dual controversial front.

The first gradual change was characterised by research in indirect instructional and observational learning, also known as modelling, by authors such as Albert Bandura (Bandura, 1997). Bandura started from a behaviourist tradition; he was the first to evidence the importance of sources of references that convey information and thus learning through modelling and not only through experiences driven by exposure to rewards or punishment, or through experiences driven by experimentation of rewarding shortcuts (Gardner, 1985a, 1985b).

In contrast, the second critical front was harder and took place in field of language comprehension and acquisition, mainly through the work of Noam Chomsky, who evidenced the main primary process of language acquisition device, which encodes language and grammatical structures within the brain, rather than considering languages as learned from environment. If anything, a specific language may be learned only due to general rules that allow us to learn one or more languages, even though they are radically different (Gardner, 1985a, 1985b).

These scientific developments have been amongst the most significant aspects of the transformation and modernisation of academic disciplines pertinent to human behaviour, and not only considering that logic, biology, and engineering have been the foundations of contemporary psychology.

Towards the end of the Fifties, research on the cognitive processes flourished; experiments were devised based on configuring psychological processes as functioning mechanisms characterised by specific laws.

Throughout this period, almost at the end of the Fifties, there was a proliferation of research on the essential constituents of the mind: experiments were devised to and aimed to configure psychological processes, as functioning mechanisms with specific laws and distinctive features. This process generated fields of enquiry, which had come to a halt, despite reaching significant conclusions regarding memory, language, reasoning.

This wave of enthusiasm, which showed promising perspectives, delineated the formulation of new practices and laws, which have almost entirely maintained their scientific validity thus far.

CBT Stemming from Clinical Treatments

The second fundamental perspective in the historical evolution of CBT is the development of procedures in the treatment of mental disorders.

Whilst in core disciplines, theoretical language strictly adhered to empirical scientific method, initially based on verificationism and subsequently falsificationism, as formulated by Karl Popper (1972), clinical disciplines generated an animated debate amongst three theoretical orientations (Dobson & Dozois, 2019).

- The organicist stance based on the developments of psychopharmacology for depression and psychoses
- Freud's psychoanalysis and his students' stance, which contributed to the understanding and formulation of mental disorders based on a person's history, and his (or hers') early attachment patterns
- The application of conditioning theories (either classic Pavlovian or operant Skinnerism), for the treatment of behavioural disorders

This is where Beck, a psychiatrist, and Ellis, a psychologist, both trained in psychoanalysis, developed cognitive behavioural treatments (Dobson & Dozois, 2019).

When working with depressed patients, Beck noticed poor outcomes when utilising traditional treatments in his clinics. He unequivocally identified cognitive features in his patients, as opposed to psychoanalysis, which focused on affective relationships in infancy. Such cognitive features are known as negative automatic thoughts and cognitive distortions.

Beck noticed that depressed patients did not experience unconscious anger as a core aspect of depression, but rather genuine pessimism, which was incessantly present in their thought processes. Beck asked his patients to say aloud what they were thinking and noticed that their statements reflected something that was different from psychoanalysis, and akin to common sense instead. These pivotal discoveries generated Cognitive Therapy (Beck, 2021).

Ellis focused on behavioural problems and psychological disorders, such as anxiety and sexual inhibition; he evidenced that patients' beliefs were characterised by unrealistic ideas. While this is common practice in therapy today, in those times, the common practice was to engage in a direct dialogue with his patients, to foster understanding of problems based on acceptance or self-encouragement to do what was best in that situation, rather than focusing on unhelpful and rigid beliefs.

Treatment goals aimed at challenging dichotomous and inflexible beliefs in the present, rather than looking at possible causes in the past.

Similarly to Beck, Ellis placed importance on change in the here and now, targeting interventions on beliefs that patients had on themselves, their environment, and the others. Such theoretical and technical rupture lead to the development of Rational Emotive Therapy or REBT.

Beck and Ellis are the main representatives of classic cognitive behavioural psychotherapy.

Authors such as Meichenbaum, Mahoney, Godfried, Rachman, and Kendall (Dobson & Dobson, 2018) subsequently approached CBT from a different theoretical and technical perspective, characterised by behavioural modification and conditioning theories; they discovered and evidenced cognitive functioning features (i.e. Meichenbaum's cognitive behaviour modification therapy; Meichenbaum, 1977) thereafter.

According to the seminal work by Alan Kazdin (1978), the term cognitive behaviour modification therapy refers to treatments that propose behavioural change through modification of thoughts, interpretations, beliefs, and responses.

CBT subsequently incorporated a few strands that were not fully integrated up until a few decades ago: Beck's Cognitive Therapy, Ellis' REBT, and other cognitive behavioural psychotherapies such as Meichenbaum's Stress Inoculation Therapy, Problem Solving Training, Social Skills

Training, Assertive Training, and a wide range of specific strategies aimed at solving problems originated by a behaviourist perspective but reinterpreted in a cognitive key (Dobson & Dozois, 2019).

CBT progressively extended the range of its therapeutic aims and interests, attempting to integrate research outcomes on early attachment and a considerable number of studies on infant research, which started from Konrad Lorenz and continued to be developed further by Bowlby, Ainsworth, and Harlow (Trull & Prinstein, 2013).

The key concept is that primary determinants of attachments and factors that influence them provide intrinsic information to the individual in building his knowledge and expectations around him. These discoveries, crucial for the understanding of childhood problems, maintain their relevance in adult psychology also (Bowlby, 1989).

As you can see, CBT has a strong lineage in integrating what has gone before into a strong emergent psychotherapy that draws on the strengths of both research and practice over many decades. This commitment to considering and responding to emerging evidence remains a key part of CBT going forward.

Current Integrative Challenges

There is an ongoing debate between Modernist Clinical Cognitivism and Post-Modern Constructivist Psychotherapies (Trull & Prinstein, 2013). The future of the debate seems directed to an integration based on common therapy features and concordance on research of cognitive processes and on effective aspects of treatments.

According to Clark (1996), there are five fundamental features that characterise the CBT model:

1 Individuals actively contribute to the development of their own reality
2 Emotions and behaviours are influenced by cognitive contents, processes, and structures, according to reciprocal determinism. Behavioural and emotional responses cannot exist without cognitive mediation
3 Even though several levels of awareness may exist and may require different degrees of attention and self-awareness, cognitive processes that mediate emotions and behaviours are accessible and recognisable
4 Cognitive change is the crucial drive to justify processes of change
5 Therapeutic intervention focus is always on changing the meaning of the evaluation of threat in contexts relevant to the life of the patient

According to Mahoney (2000), there might be over 20 theoretical approaches in CBT, approaches that have common emphasis on structures of meaning and information processing (Semerari, 2000).

Lastly, it is seldom emphasised that CBT is more than just psychological treatment for a wide range of mental disorders. CBT provides us with a wealth of information to understand behaviour. Currently we cannot separate it from cognitive psychology and its applications in several aspects of our daily lives (Zimmerman & Schunk, 2003). In fact, CBT incorporated multiple aspects stemming from research and its application, along with empirically validated treatment protocols, which combined different fields, i.e., psychology of cognitive processes, psychophysiology, informatics, and social psychology.

Conclusion

CBT is founded on the importance of change of thought contents and processes, and as such of meaning we attribute to events and the information that surround us. Personal meaning that is created and developed by individuals becomes crucial, as it represents the foundation for expectations, hypotheses, inferences, and pursuit of meaningful goals.

Our personal perspective, from which we contextualise information, is influenced by environmental and relational contexts; this aspect becomes extremely significant when we consider how information is utilised to appraise situations or evaluate our actions.

Cognitive Therapy is Constructivist in this sense, as it places at the core of its premises development of meaning and emphasis on its subjective appraisal more than on reality in its purest form. Furthermore, Cognitive Therapy currently places at the core of its conceptualisation of individual problems the dissatisfaction resulting from lack of achievement of meaningful goals.

In this context, Cognitive Theory links motivation theory and psychology of the emotions with evolutionary psychology (Barlow, 2008; Beck, 1996; Gilbert, 2014; Seligman & Csikszentmihalyi, 2000; Young, Klosko, & Weishaar, 2003).

CBT cannot be considered differently from Cognitive Therapy, as CBT fully incorporates all the aspects of Beck's Cognitive Therapy; in fact, the latter has the undeniable lead as a standard treatment for most psychological disorders (Beck, 2021).

The authors consider CBT as the psychotherapeutic treatment of choice, with appropriate modifications, when required, by specific empirically validated protocols. We hope it will be evident throughout this book that the utilisation of CBT as core psychotherapy lends itself to integration.

CBT is at the service not only of an integration of several treatment techniques, previously kept separated by rigid theoretical orientations, but also to perspectives linked to early cognitive schemas, therapeutic relationship, and its conscious and unconscious dynamics, to individuals' values which influence life directions and acceptance of what is not within the power and the responsibility of the individual.

The message that we can comprehend, relate, and remedy psychological suffering is an example of the contribution we endeavour to provide.

The integrative stance proposed by our work leads to linking CBT with fields farther away from it, such as counselling, and psychological training in working environments.

Why have we written this book? The importance of having an overview of what works best and contributing to a better understanding of clinical cases in psychotherapy stimulated us to reflect on other kinds of challenges linked between each other. What is the relationship between CBT and its philosophical foundations? What influence have patients' conceptualisations on what characterises their own suffering? What kind of values in a patient's life represent a background to psychotherapeutic work? How can we explain certain psychological traps and vicious circles, for the purpose of an effective and efficacious therapy?

All these questions and many other considerations in our work stimulated and encouraged us to clarify several aspects, which we felt were not well positioned within a singular CBT approach.

Our answers spontaneously converged towards an integrative direction with a common core indicated for various treatments and theories considered including those that stretched beyond the CBT therapies such as Standard CBT, ACT, Schema Therapy, Mindfulness-Based CBT, and Brief Psychodynamic Psychotherapy; an approach in keeping with assimilative integration.

We all felt comfortable, despite our existing differences, using an integrative CBT perspective, as it gave us freedom of mind to direct it to our specific interests.

References

American Psychological Association. (2006). Evidence-based practice in psychology. APA presidential task force on evidence-based practice in psychology. *American Psychologist, 61*, 271–285.

Bandura, A. (1997). *Self-efficacy: The exercise of control.* New York, NY: W.H. Freeman, Times Books. Henry Holt & Co.

Barlow, D.H. (2008). *Clinical handbook of psychological disorders: A step-by-step treatment manual.* New York, NY: Guilford Press.

Beck, A.T. (1996). Beyond belief: A theory of modes, personality, and psychopathology. In P.M. Salkovskis (Ed.), *Frontiers of cognitive therapy* (pp. 1–25). New York, NY: Guilford Press.

Beck, J. (2021). *Cognitive behavioral therapy* (3rd ed.). New York, NY: Guilford Press.

Bowlby, J. (1989). The role of attachment in personality development and psychopathology. In S. I. Greenspan & G. H. Pollock (Eds.), *The course of life, Vol. 1. Infancy* (pp. 229–270). Madison, US: International Universities Press, Inc. (Reprinted from "American Journal of Psychiatry," 1987, Vol. 144; and from "American Journal of Orthopsychiatry," 1982, Vol. 52).

Clark, D.M. (1996). Panic disorder: From theory to therapy. In P.M. Salkovskis (Ed.), *Frontiers of cognitive therapy*. New York, NY: Guilford Press.

David, D., Cristea, I., & Hofman, S.G. (2018). Why cognitive behavioural therapy is the current gold standard of psychotherapy? *Frontiers in Psychiatry, 9*, 4.

Dobson, D., & Dobson, K.S. (2018). *Evidence-based practice of cognitive behavioral therapy*. New York, NY: Guilford Press.

Dobson, K.S., & Dozois, D.J.A. (2019). *Handbook of cognitive-behavioral therapies*. New York, NY: Guilford Press.

Emmelkamp, P.M., David, D., Beckers, T., Muris, P., Cuijpers, P., Lutz, W., ... Vervliet, B. (2014). Advancing psychotherapy and evidence-based psychological interventions. *International Journal of Methods in Psychiatric Research, 23*(Suppl. 1), 58–91.

Gardner, H. (1985a). *The mind's new science*. New York, NY: Basic Books.

Gardner, R.C. (1985b). *Social psychology and second language learning: The role of attitudes and motivation*. London: Edward Arnold.

Gilbert, P. (2014). The origins and nature of compassion focused therapy. *British Journal of Clinical Psychology, 79*(5), 618–628.

Huhn, M., Tardy, M., Spineli, L.M., Kissling, W., Förstl, H., Pitschel-Walz, G., ... Leucht, S. (2014). Efficacy of pharmacotherapy and psychotherapy for adult psychiatric disorders: A systematic overview of meta-analyses. *JAMA Psychiatry, 71*, 706–715.

Kazdin, A.E. (1978). *Behavior modification in applied settings*. New York, NY: Waveland Press.

Kazdin, A.E. (2008). Evidence-based treatment and practice: New opportunities to bridge clinical research and practice, enhance the knowledge base, and improve patient care. *American Psychologist, 63*, 146–159.

Legrenzi, P. (2019). *Storia della psicologia* (6th ed.). Bologna: Il Mulino.

Mahoney, J. (2000). Path dependence in historical sociology. *Theory and Society, 29*(4), 507–548. http://www.jstor.org/stable/3108585

Meichenbaum, D.H. (1977). *Cognitive behaviour modification: An integrative approach*. New York, NY: Plenum.

Norcross, J.C., & Goldfried, M.R. (2019). *Handbook of psychotherapy integration* (3rd ed.). New York, NY: Oxford University Press.

Popper, K. (1972). *Conjectures and refutations* (4th ed.). London: Routledge.

Sakaluk, J.K., Williams, A.J., Kilshaw, R.E., & Rhyner, K.T. (2019). Evaluating the evidential value of empirically supported psychological treatments (ESTs): A meta-scientific review. *Journal of Abnormal Psychology, 128*(6), 500–509. doi:10.1037/abn0000421

Seligman, M.E.P., & Csikszentmihalyi, M. (2000). Positive psychology: An introduction. *American Psychologist, 55*(1), 5–14. doi:10.1037/0003-066X.55.1.5

Semerari, A. (2000). *Storia, teorie e tecniche della psicoterapia cognitiva*. Bari-Roma: Laterza.

Sturmey, P., & Hersen, M. (2012). *Handbook of evidence based practice in clinical psychology*. Hoboken, NJ: Wiley.

Trull, T.J., & Prinstein, M.J. (2013). *Clinical psychology* (8th ed.). Wadsworth, OH: Cengage Learning.

Young, J., Klosko, J.S., & Weishaar, M.E. (2003). *Schema therapy. A practitioner's guide*. New York, NY: Guilford Press.

Zimmerman, B.J., & Schunk, D.H. (Eds.). (2003). *Educational psychology: A century of contributions*. Mahwah, NJ: Erlbaum.

Chapter 1

Importance of Integrative Psychotherapy

1.1 Significance of Integrative Psychotherapy

An incipit is often the most challenging aspect of a book, as there are so many expectations about beginnings. The beginning of a literary work is considered a business card, a curriculum vitae. Instinctively, we would like to argue that Cognitive Behavioural Therapy (CBT) is the Integrative Psychotherapy that psychotherapists have always yearned and aspired to have in their toolbox.

Psychotherapy integration is an advanced and rigorous academic field, and is a part of the American Psychological Association (APA).

It is like the Holy Grail: CBT has been extensively appraised and evaluated from a theoretical and evidence-based perspective.

We are not referring to specific kinds of CBT, for instance, Beck's *Cognitive Therapy* (2011) or Young's *Schema Therapy* (Young, Klosko, & Weishaar, 2003), and even less to specific and sectarian CBT models. We are referring to CBT as a wider category. CBT could be conceived as a kind of psychotherapy or psychotherapies set that have common characteristics, the ABC model, for instance, cognitive theory of emotions, learning paradigms, focus on individual's subjective perspectives that create focus on aims and knowledge, and cognitive and metacognitive competencies.

A novel element is represented by the progressive detachment from categorical models driven by concordance with DSM5 (2012); that is, each diagnostic category corresponds to a formulation and specific treatment. This approach has entered a profound crisis, due to poor external validity of diagnostic categories and conversely due to a progressive development of transdiagnostic processes and macro-categories of psychopathological factors. Thus, psychotherapy has started to consider themes and processes that share common characteristics in relation to specific disorders: this process is implemented through cross-sectional modalities. What emerges from this scenario is a psychotherapy more recognisable and familiar to most psychotherapists from different training and backgrounds; psychotherapeutic resources and

DOI: 10.4324/9781003299226-2

language developed are readily shareable, due to common foundations and modalities, which are familiar to the most experienced psychotherapists.

For example, let us focus on individuals suffering from generalised anxiety disorder (GAD). In this context, we may identify a number of psychological factors and processes, which are variably subjective and GAD specific, but may be shared at the same time with a group of individuals who have been diagnosed with anxiety disorder, who have elements in common with individuals suffering from depression, and subsequent common psychopathological features with individuals who suffer from other diagnoses.

Individuals suffering from GAD are likely to be concerned with adversities, tend to ruminate and seek reassurance, avoid anxiety-provoking situations, and will engage in avoidant safety behaviours to protect themselves from anxiety.

Thus, a category-driven diagnosis might not provide useful information other than the level of impairment related to specific symptoms. The majority of psychological processes and dysfunctional beliefs and assumptions have shared features in individuals who have been diagnosed with anxiety disorders; this is because of common aims that are pursued as part of the disorder (i.e. avoidance strategies).

But there is more. There is a clear research trend that indicates a certain continuity and overlap between disorders of different nature, such as anxiety and depressive disorders, conduct and personality disorders, and to a certain extent, psychotic disorders (Barlow, Allen, & Choate, 2004). Psychological problems might be interpreted as having shared and well-defined coping processes: these can be explained by the fact that human beings share common intents which, if frustrated, threatened, or unfulfilled, trigger psychological suffering. Integrative Psychotherapy represents a perspective shared by colleagues worldwide, a framework that helps to resolve long-standing problems and safety behaviours is a common ground within many psychotherapeutic approaches.

Integrative Psychotherapy models developed so far, Cognitive Behavioural Analysis System of Psychotherapy (CBASP; McCullough, 2000), for instance, have been developed combining CBT, interpersonal psychotherapy (IPT; Weissman, Markowitz, & Klerman, 2018), and psychodynamic therapy models. These approaches offer therapeutic tools based on evidence-based models, which may be utilised to meet the needs of chronically depressed patients who do not respond to classic CBT or IPT. An Integrative Psychotherapy model offers interventions that might be able to address and solve problems related to technical language and evidence-based procedures, whilst fulfilling the requirement of a unified clinical formulation of patients' problems. This is a complex task despite the significant amount of work that has been attempted to address this problem. Such a task is complex, but not impossible.

Diagnosis is important, but it is only the beginning. A good formulation is an essential requirement; an integrative perspective aims to address macro-psychological processes, rather than specific categories described in DSM-5: these don't seem to be useful and have internal and external validity (Hayes, Hofmann, & Ciarocchi, 2020).

This conceptualisation may appear simplistic; however, it represents a useful example to focus and underline the main role of evaluation that individuals give to events, and if whatever happens is justifiable in line with their own existence or values. For instance: am I being wronged? Can I take a certain risk and deal with the related consequences? In what way does all this make sense to me?

We all look for justifications and reasons. We often wonder as to how we can find ways to make sense of what happens to us, should this even be a random justification that all that happens around us is random.

In this context, it is useful not to lose sight of the role that "secondary problems" have; later on (Chapter 4), we will examine this construct and its remarkable significance. One of the main characteristics of problems is to regulate our sense of self-protection from consequences of frustration, in line with a specific problem.

Processes such as rumination, avoidance, self-criticism, lack of motivation, risk-taking behaviours, reassurance-seeking behaviours, abusive behaviours, self-enhancement, and overconfidence are all secondary psychological processes and conceptualised as coping strategies, developed to manage frustration. A balanced perspective would be to tolerate frustration, attributing a realistic perspective, and focus on problem-solving strategies.

It is important to consider that a considerable portion of these coping strategies might be vaguely avoidant in nature. Social learning would suffice in creating a context where avoiding our own experiences, and lack of acceptance of negative emotions, may be rapidly developed (Barlow, 2002).

Usually the starting point of avoidance is the natural propensity of every living organism to avoid an aversive stimulus, that is, for instance, pain.

The environment and contexts in which we live regulate our inclinations, whereas the expectation of pain pushes us in the opposite direction (Barlow, 2022). Thus, the here and now, "present" contexts, represent the foundation of flexibility; it is learning, which is consistently operating in an ongoing process, which fluctuates between an experience in the present moment and our expectations.

Avoidance of inner experience and the price to pay for ongoing psychological life and learning are conceptualised as vulnerability factors within any form of psychopathology. Avoidance, well before becoming a specific behaviour, in a specific context or environment, soon becomes a generalisable rule. Avoidance, as a rule, superintends in a generalised way individuals' responses. It is a rule that is learned and confirmed by specific behaviours (negative reinforcement traps and confirmation of unhelpful hypotheses) (Barlow, 2022; Beck, 2011).

If we reverse the conceptualisation of avoidance, what we might discover is specific acceptance of something in a certain context (something that is not within our power or control), and of acceptance as a generalised rule (knowledge that we accept something is not within our control). Albert Ellis argued that individuals have a propensity to believe that they should never suffer or experience frustration: this drives certain avoidance strategies and assumptions (Dobson & Dozois, 2010).

Seneca and Epictetus (Robertson, 2019) come to mind: they encouraged their students to consider that all we have is a temporary loan from a creditor, Nature, which is what is external to us, and to be cautious when we are trying to do our best.

1.2 Good Diagnosis Is Just the Beginning

A clinical diagnosis is always a good starting point for psychotherapeutic interventions (Dell'Erba, 2008). A diagnosis presents unequivocal advantages. Symptoms' categorisation, behaviours, and perceptual and cognitive processes are characterised by descriptive logic and by a practical utilisation of diagnosis. However, the problem lies in the diagnostic system, which may be ambiguous and imprecise.

Diagnosis and formulation are conceptually different clinical tools. Diagnosis is important within a clinical context, for instance, in the context of eating disorders, when it is challenging to immediately proceed to formulation due to physical and cognitive problems posed by starvation. Diagnosis is constrained in its applications, particularly within current DSM-5 diagnostic categories, which have limited internal and external validity. Formulation supports a deeper understanding of individuals' differences and considers them as essential factors and variables useful in psychological interventions (Hayes et al., 2020).

Disadvantages in diagnosis are posed by significant comorbidity, and overlap between diagnostic categories, thus resulting in utilising two or three diagnostic labels, to better and satisfactorily define the individual's symptoms, along with the almost complete absence of aetiological categories.

Within medical science, a diagnostic classification disconnected from aetiology is unhelpful. This is different in psychology: developing an understanding in this area is crucial, and it might make the difference (Mancini, Mancini, & Castelfranchi, 2022). From a clinical psychology perspective, a classification of disorder based on descriptive, atheoretical categories, in a phenomenological manner, is useful although complementary in nature. The remaining aspects of the clinical picture are defined within the identification and formulation of psychological problems, within a mutual collaboration between the individual and the psychotherapist.

Case formulation or clinical conceptualisation of the case is the necessary integration between descriptive classification and guidelines for effective treatment.

A descriptive diagnosis, void of conceptualisation, might expose the individual to a "prescription" that would have little to do with the psychological distress experienced by the individual in the first instance. A clinical case formulation requires clinical psychopathology competencies, along with the knowledge of the disorders' model and within the therapeutic approach derived from a given theoretical model (CBT, psychodynamic, systemic-relational, and humanistic).

In summary, DSM5 (2012) is probably more useful to clinical psychologists and medical doctors, if diagnosis is linked to psychological formulation of the problem. It is also worth considering that DSM-5 (2012) flaws may lead to novel trans-diagnostic paths, within a psychotherapeutic approach based on clinical evidence, such as CBT.

1.3 Integrative Psychotherapy

Several aspects of our minds' activity and numerous interventions aimed to address such aspects have a trans-theoretical flavour (Hayes et al., 2020). There is a general framework that may be considered from a CBT perspective. However, there is an ongoing "hybridisation" of constructs, which are linked to other psychological perspectives. This appears to be innovative (Hayes et al., 2020).

There are some aspects of CBT that present with features similar to other theoretical approaches and that are likely to facilitate integration of theoretical and experiential frameworks. One of these concepts is the Interpersonal Schema or Mode, as theorised by Beck and subsequently by Jeffrey Young, or Pattern, as considered in Luborsky's *Brief Psychodynamic Therapy* (Luborsky & Mark, 2015) or *Brief Dynamic Interpersonal Therapy* (Lemma, Target, & Fonagy, 2011) and Ryles' *Cognitive Analytical Therapy* (1995).

There is momentum towards convergence amongst eminent psychotherapeutic traditions, despite some dissimilarities (Hayes & Hofmann, 2018). There is an increasing number of clinical psychologists that are seeking a common language, along with authors who are experimenting with theoretical frameworks; be these frameworks may be conceptualised from cognitivists and psychoanalytic perspectives and from clinicians who have a humanist counselling perspective (Stricker, 2001). Some concepts are fundamental and play a unifying and cohesive function; the concept of Pattern, for instance. An integrative attempt is characterised by an ongoing reference to approaches such as Schema Therapy, Brief Psychodynamic Psychotherapy, and CBT.

The model's CBT core construct is a Pattern, defined as unresolved problems that require further understanding and conceptualisation within an ego-syntonic narrative framework.

- First step is to identify the Pattern
- Second step is to understand the Pattern
- Third step is to opt for a perspective that differs from the Pattern
- Fourth point is to rebuild Pattern foundation
- Fifth point is to act despite the Pattern
- Sixth point is to integrate the Pattern to aspects relevant to our patients

There is a partial overlap between the above features of Pattern. Concordance with the aspects of Pattern identified is essential to the achievement of therapeutic interventions.

CBT is the theoretical reference framework, and specifically a therapy attentive to active modalities of cognitive schemas and a wide spectrum of unhelpful – dysfunctional – coping strategies.

Several models refer to non-integrated modalities towards which there is resistance and not accepted by therapists (Carcione, Niccolò, & Semerari, 2016). Lack of acceptance and experiential avoidance determine the way in which intrusive thoughts affect conscious processes, and interference with goals. Furthermore, part of individuals' aims are functional aspects of avoidance and have as a consequence further distancing from meaningful goals.

In this instance, conflicts are configured between goals that pursue avoidance of cognitive schemas and experiences and goals that aim to achieve values, as part of our identity and personal growth.

Therapy aims to facilitate autobiographical identification and comprehension of Pattern, and its acceptance is in line with a previous and yet different meaning, thus valuing achievement of meaningful aims and intents, whilst maintaining motivation.

CBT interventions such as analytical distancing, cognitive restructuring, hypotheses testing, and exposure play a crucial role in changing perspective and restructuring cognitive content as a material that can be utilised to reframe past experiences.

Theoretical approaches that are identified at the core of such intervention invoke Dynamic Psychotherapy, and most importantly, Interpersonal Psychoanalysis, Schema Therapy, Cognitive Analytical Therapy, and part of Cognitive Therapy linked to Interpersonal Schemas are linked to the latter (Carcione et al., 2016; Cooper & McLeod, 2011; Denman, 2001; Ryle, 1995).

On the other hand, we find inspiration from other therapeutic orientations that value metacognition, as well as goals pursued by individuals along with both his normal and dysfunctional conflicts.

The current integrative attempt has empirical value, as it is stemming from clinical work and produced effective outcomes (Norcross, 2012; Norcross & Goldfried, 2019). It is useful to the understanding of the individual problems in work aimed at psychological change, and a theoretical purpose (i.e. trying to consolidate constructs, processes, and interventions considered valid and effective).

It is plausible to consider an integrative formulation, aimed at capturing patterns and emphasising behaviours that focus on avoiding suffering, to encourage identification and change of dysfunctional coping strategies within a trans-theoretical perspective.

Validating patients' coping strategies to distance themselves from psychological suffering seems a further step towards a more in-depth understanding of patients.

A clinical formulation framework may be characterised by several dimensions, as there may be several aspects that might be considered by a therapist, both from a descriptive and an operational strategic perspective.

In a manner inspired by an integrative perspective, we can formulate ideas of dealing with distress and psychological suffering, and ways in which we attempt to respond to challenges posed by our lives, at the core of psychological formulation.

A mutual understanding of the Pattern and interpersonal responses seems a core feature for CBT and Psychodynamic Psychotherapy.

The following figure captures Pattern integration in psychotherapy. It attempts to utilise constructs that are common to most theoretical approaches.

1.4 Individual Goals vs Therapist Goals

Sometimes we misinterpret what our patients seek, their goals, and the psychotherapists' strategies. For instance, assumptions and subjective rules aimed at not suffering are simplified.

A psychotherapist would like to support his/her patients to live better and not simply feel better.

Nevertheless, there is a therapeutic commitment to deal with patients' problems; a psychotherapist might fail to discern between what can be achieved (and within this to identify meaningful therapy goals with the patient) and what the patient seeks, i.e. not to suffer without any further elaboration.

Clinical work could not only be symptom focused. A wider perspective when working clinically is recommended, as clinical work may not be just focused on symptoms. A therapist might collude with inflexible dysfunctional rules and assumptions, and avoidant strategies should therapeutic work be symptom focused. It is worthwhile to consider that what might be affected is not our emotional state, but goals and aims instead. In this context, psychotherapy would inevitably become a dysfunctional avoidance strategy.

Feelings, anxiety in particular, become clinical conditions when individuals struggle to accept their own inner experiences. People might struggle to tend to their own feelings and intentionally attempt to alter their own experience, thus developing a potentially inflexible cognitive style and thus paying a high price at the personal and interpersonal level. Any sacrifice, any loss may involve pain and frustration. However, it is possible that, when accepting normal feelings of powerlessness, thus recalibrating aims and goals within our control, we battle sacrifice and frustration as emotional states. All this is likely to come at a high cost.

Psychotherapy focuses on improving our ability to experience our feelings towards better living our life, rather than engaging in life to feel good and to experience positive feelings and emotions. Thus, living better rather than feeling better.

We transform suffering through acceptance (see Chapter 6), which otherwise would not be tolerated, into pain that can be tolerated; suffering becomes pain, which is part of life. The whole focus of possible and meaningful intents makes a difference.

1.5 Stereotypes and Popularisation in Psychotherapy

There are several aspects of psychotherapy that require further clarification and development. We will focus on the idea that people have about psychotherapy, as a means to help themselves through therapeutic work with a psychotherapist. This is a complex issue.

It is hard to determine exactly how psychotherapy is depicted, socially or conceptually, with regard to several clinical approaches. It may be challenging to make sense of constructs that are anchored on generic psychological features, such as emotions, the mind, behaviours, values, cognitive processes, and stress.

Similarly, it may be arduous to formulate the differences between professional roles that gravitate around psychotherapy, such as psychologists, psychiatrists, and psychotherapists. This is due to ever so rapid cultural and cross-cultural changes.

In fact, a hypothetical socio-psychological research study designed to understand psychotherapy and its influence on individuals would capture a snapshot of an ever-changing phenomenon, which is rapidly and unpredictably evolving.

There might be a discrepancy between professional and psychotherapeutic practice, and the opinions and expectations of non-experts. Often, news reports, for instance, refer to psychological constructs and concepts not always scientifically founded, with naïve explanations offered by opinion makers, which are expressed in a spurious psychological language.

For example, the tendency to utilise language based on neuroscience, a "neuromania," to quote Paolo Legrenzi (Legrenzi & Umiltà, 2009), rather than accessible language, with pure, unadulterated psychological concepts at its core.

1.6 Dissemination of Standard Procedures in Psychotherapy

When we focus on dissemination of psychology, on concepts of psychological practice and psychotherapy, we notice that there is a myriad of information that encourages the reader to free himself of negative emotions and become happy and fulfilled. This might lead to misinformation about psychotherapy interventions aimed at addressing unhelpful thinking styles.

Self-help books as a genre provide advice and aim at persuading individuals to free themselves of negative emotions, such as anxiety, sadness, anger, negative thoughts, and self-criticism, physical symptoms associated with unpleasant sensations within our functioning as human beings (Hayes, Strosahl, & Wilson, 2011). Following this direction without critically appraising it might mean to develop a false sense of happiness, a myth of serenity and well-being, as absence of nuisances and stress that is frankly not realistic.

In fact, had it been possible to eradicate biological mechanisms that are at the basis of our emotions, the result would be being no longer human, thus intolerable for anyone. We focus on the relentless pursuit against stressful situations and emotions, because we are disinclined to experience affliction and everything that is not in keeping with our desires. The true drive that activates us is frustration, which is an integral part of our lives.

1.7 The Psychotherapy Craze

Many current and past psychotherapeutic approaches have striven to help individuals to suffer less by offering interventions based on distractions and ways to exercise control over emotions. Those interventions should support to "correct" or "change" negative thoughts, helping them to contrast experiences that, although negative, are involuntary or unintentional (Dobson, 2010). All of this, throughout the years, had become a precious heritage, a sort of collection of failure, which is standing as a legacy of disastrous and erroneous attempts geared on feeling better.

It is becoming clearer, currently, that "feeling better" is not the ultimate goal, and occasionally, it is a short-term goal, the problem, rather than the destination or the solution (Hayes & Hofmann, 2018; Hayes et al., 2011).

We understand better with a little nudge from contemporary philosophy (Robertson, 2019), inspired by the great classic philosophy ideas, that what seems to be important to individuals is an ideal direction, a value, a destination, and a meaning, rather than physical or emotional states (make money, feel good, take drugs, own a Ferrari, or become a supervisor or CEO) (McKay, Forsyth, & Eifert, 2010).

A goal, however important, career progression or a new home, represents a step that fulfils its potential once it has been achieved, whereas values linked to individuals' meaning are deeply connected with our well-being (Diener, 1984; Diener & Diener, 1995; Diener, Lucas, & Scollon, 2006).

Several advanced clinical treatments, effective in the treatment of psychiatric disorders, no longer have the purpose to achieve a supposedly abstract state of normality, well-being, or happiness. Such criterion is more and more focused on providing tools to individuals so they can direct them towards the sense of direction that is important to them, and empower them, as much as possible, to choose. All these interventions are usually based on normal working psychological processes, such as experiences, consciousness, abstraction, choices, awareness, and commitment.

1.8 Cognitive Behavioural Psychotherapy as a Synthesis

In the field of interventions for clinical disorders and psychotherapies, treatments considered more effective, both in the vast majority of rigorously controlled studies (with well selected patients) and in the controlled studies of routine clinical practice of local psychotherapy services (patients not selected), are treatments derived from Cognitive Behavioural Psychotherapy. Cognitive Behavioural Psychotherapy is a wide range of interventions and treatments that include therapies and models that may appear different from each other. However, a common denominator remains a crucial aspect, not only in psychology but also in the history of all human thought, from Ancient Greece to today: behaviour is usually driven by information related to goals; emotions are generally the result of evaluations, whether we are aware of them or not, regarding frustrations or acquisitions of goals (Alford & Beck, 1997).

This commonality, which is part of all CBT therapies, is shared by previous clinical orientations of psychology and psychotherapy. In fact, in the current panorama, the trend that seems to appear more pronounced is the integration between CBT and other psychological theories and therapies, in a more updated and sophisticated version. According to some authors (Borgo, Sibilia, & Marks, 2015), there are approximately 500 different psychotherapeutic approaches: this is a chaotic and intricate realm, challenging to comprehend for inexperienced therapists.

Within these approaches, there are many, but not as many as it may seem, that utilise a different language, for the same psychological aspects (Gilbert & Orlans, 2010).

Arguably, no effective psychotherapy is truly exempt from CBT's main features (Borgo et al., 2015). This might come as a surprise, when we consider Psychoanalysis, which represents, in our collective imagination, the quintessence of psychotherapy.

Nevertheless, all of the recent models derived from Psychoanalysis, and the thoughts of several psychoanalytic authors, reflect this very issue: several aspects of CBT have been integrated to their technical toolbox and therefore progressed within the hierarchy of recommended evidence-based psychotherapeutic treatments.

There are, however, crucial internal differences within the CBT field, such as the following:

- Identification of psychological processes
- Self-awareness or metacognition of cognitive processes
- Focus on evaluative processes and whether related focus on them is useful or conversely dysfunctional to take them for granted, for the well-being and healthy individuals' functioning
- The role played by attention and by awareness of perception and observation. A more detached stance compared to readiness to change, solve, or process behavioural strategies
- Cognitive processes linked to problem-solving, and evaluation of beliefs and judgements that can be characterised as "top-down" processes, which are distinct from perception of reality or adherence to stimuli
- Of crucial importance is the focus placed on the evaluative role on the goals, or consideration of the pursuit of a specific goal: what is the meaning attributed to a threat that might affect a given goal?

These are some aspects of what CBT has acquired from other disciplines and that CBT has indirectly promoted in other therapeutic modalities (i.e. exposure and social skills training).

The model that we may, hypothetically, approach in the future is a model with a CBT core, but is characterised by hybrid interventions and techniques derived from several psychotherapies, which have become conceptually different from tangential or integrated representations.

1.9 Psychology Based on Model Fidelity vs Pseudo Psychology

There are differences between well-presented, corroborated, and evidence-based psychological and pseudo psychological models, the latter being hardly coherent, absurd, and incomprehensible.

Within the wide variety of psychological models and theories, there are some perspectives that we might consider complicated and difficult to comprehend.

CBT seems to be the best available theoretical framework for psychotherapy integration, as it possesses the ingredients to incorporate the best of other available approaches, whilst integrating without major conceptual problems therapeutic interventions; this is evident in various meta-analyses and outcome studies (see Sakaluk, Williams, Kilshaw, & Rhyner, 2019).

There is a frequent and current stance that consists in placing emphasis on self-convenience.

The linchpin of such a widespread stance, not only between non-experts but also between professionals whether clinical psychologists or psychiatrists, is that it would be "convenient" to experience, or not to experience, certain intentional mental states such as beliefs, intentions, and desires (Dell'Erba & Nuzzo, 2010; Miceli & Castelfranchi, 2014).

It is common to encounter in cognitive behavioural analyses and explanations that are based on the concept of "self-convenience."

These argumentations are utilised in several contexts, such as attitudes towards emotions (anxiety, anger, and depression) or evaluation of our worry, or adopting schemas related to self or related to specific aspects of the self: in all of these cases, self-convenience is often evoked as a decisional standard, or as an explanatory causation.

Let us consider some examples. When individuals are preoccupied with a future threat, an illness, a bereavement, or a loss, they might be tense and will interpret this preoccupation as necessary to prevent such future threats.

Utilisation of self-convenience is a common element that explains preoccupation, as the means to feel less anxious: this is an unfounded argument, void of psychological foundation.

Whilst it is plausible to believe that persisting in a ruminative and preoccupied state, and imagining a threatening scenario, can minimise the likelihood of such a threat (and this is understandable, although the consequences are dysfunctional), the same persistence in pursuing rumination cannot be linked to self-convenience. Individuals cannot pretend to believe in something, or as a means to achieve a purpose, but they believe this as it is plausible to them. It might be challenging, and yet plausible for some individuals to hold beliefs as means to achieve a purpose.

This is a common and popular fallacy, not only in psychology, i.e. in William James' Psychologist's Fallacy, but also in philosophy in Plato's Allegory of the Cave (Warburton, 2007).

In fact, "self-convenience" is often utilised within problem-solving, as if examining the advantages or disadvantages can lead to a resolutive decision, on themes that are pertinent and close to our own emotions, our own schemas, our own worries, and our own mental states (Mele, 2001).

The analysis of advantages and disadvantages of the problem could help to decide and clarify the nature of the problem. However, a decision made on the advantages and disadvantages related to our own beliefs, or experiencing certain feelings, or being as part of certain mental states, seems absurd and inadmissible.

A person might not consider this argument or utilise it to modify unhelpful beliefs, nor utilise it to mitigate or modify their own mental states. Individuals that believe they are failures commonly do not change their mind because this belief represents a disadvantage. In fact, such disadvantage is often considered a further pejorative element and leads to further de-evaluation and desperation.

This is an unhelpful way of thinking about psychology, as it might be deceiving. It is equally absurd to focus on the advantage (or disadvantage) of believing something; or to believe or not believe for the advantage (or the disadvantage) (Davidson, 1987).

Believing or not believing in something could be advantageous or disadvantageous, but this evaluation places itself at a different level, a "meta-evaluative" level, with the benefit of hindsight, and is disconnected to the actual awareness of the problems that individuals perceive or imagine.

An atheist, for instance, may admit that believing in God would result in him feeling less lonely and vulnerable, but he would still remain an atheist.

A further analogy would be to show an atheist research that proves that believers are happier, healthier, and handsome: such evidence would not result in a shift in his beliefs.

To conclude, we would like to reflect that several techniques of analysis and modification of evaluation of the individual, based on what is convenient, i.e. "think something or something different," not only are not effective, but also represent fertile foundation for the development of new problems, discovery of new faults and failures, in that these tasks are impossible and they become problems.

There is evidence that being married is correlated to better health, and to a reduced occurrence of cardiovascular problems, compared to single individuals (Becciu & Colasanti, 2016). However, no one would marry, in order not to have a heart attack, and no one would recommend marriage due to such evidence.

Such is the problem of optimism. Optimistic individuals have better health, and better quality of life. But who can become an optimist to have better health?

A further example is posed by forgiveness. The ability to forgive is linked to better health and reduced likelihood of occurrence of depression (Boniwell, 2016). However, who can forgive someone just to be in better health or not to be depressed?

There are a multitude of professionals that pursue this deception, without reflecting on these arguments (Legrenzi, 2019). Although it might seem unusual, several psychologists and psychiatrists are influenced by what William James (1950), defined as Psychologist's Fallacy.

The *great* snare of the psychologist is the *confusion of his own standpoint with that of the mental fact* about which he is making his report. The psychologist stands outside of the mental state he speaks of. Both itself and its object are objects for him. Now when it is a *cognitive* state (percept, thought, concept, etc.), he ordinarily has no other way of naming it than as the thought, percept, etc., *of that object.* He himself meanwhile, knowing the self-same object in *his* way, gets easily led to suppose that the thought, which is *of* it, knows it in the same way in which he knows it, although this is often very far from being the case.

The assumption is that the mental state studied should be conscious of itself as the psychologist is conscious of it.

The experience of the individual is thus disregarded in favour of hypotheses, which are external to the experience of the individual; such hypotheses require technical knowledge that is counter-intuitive for the individual. Some therapists often tend to not consider the individuals' experience and provide erroneous, misleading formulations. Fortunately, this does not occur often. We might argue that objective evaluation of advantages or disadvantages in believing in something provides cues on the strategies that we could implement, in order not to analytically evaluate a certain fact in a detailed way, and the strength of our beliefs. This is not a direct but a mediated process (Davidson, 1987).

We reflected on how psychotherapeutic interventions and psychological approaches are disseminated, often in an oversimplified manner, based on the concept of convenience. Although CBT has established itself as a psychotherapy based on synthesis and is integrated to other psychotherapeutic approaches and vice versa, its simplification and "convenience" lead to fallacies, already outlined by William James, and generate "psychology craze," based on reducing suffering and creating therapeutic shifts.

We explore how CBT tools, and the way they conceptualise emotions, position CBT at the core of an ideal Integrative Psychotherapy.

1.10 Case Example

Ivan was a 33-year-old man, an only child of parents who were retired council employees.

Ivan earned a degree in communication studies and was employed by a marketing agency on a fixed term contract. Ivan had not kept in contact with his friends and was sporadically in touch with two or three peers, his closest friends from secondary school.

Ivan was in a relationship with Marta, a 26-year-old biology student, in a university out of Ivan's area.

Ivan presented with a long-standing history of panic attacks, recurring generalised worries, and prolonged spells of depressed mood.

Ivan was seen by three different psychiatrists in rapid succession: he did not receive any benefits from a pharmacological treatment based on a combination of SSRIs and benzodiazepines. A year later, Ivan sought input from a psychodynamic psychotherapist and underwent 6 months of therapy. He subsequently stopped psychotherapy, as he did not find it beneficial.

Ivan sought further psychotherapeutic input with one of the authors (GLD). Psychological assessment findings were in keeping with GAD and dependent personality traits.

Further psychological assessment findings highlighted safety behaviours such as avoidance, reassurance-seeking behaviours, procrastination, rumination, and poor self-esteem.

A core aspect of GLD's collaborative formulation shared with Ivan was that his core beliefs were centred on the intense preoccupation of not being able to cope on his own, without a strong significant other beside him. Ivan envisaged a life on his own: a cognitive schema of dependence, incompetence, and undeveloped self.

As psychotherapy progressed, it was evident that Ivan was seeking his psychotherapist's advice and comfort. This pattern was openly explored with Ivan and linked to his early experiences, as a way of distancing from his younger self-perspective, in relation to his adult self in session.

Understanding and identification of coping dysfunctional strategies was the beginning of Ivan's improvement of clinical symptoms.

References

Alford, B., & Beck, A.T. (1997). *The integrative power of cognitive therapy*. New York, NY: Guilford Press.

Barlow D.H. (2002). *Anxiety and its disorders* (2nd ed.). New York, NY: Guilford Press.

Barlow, D.H. (Ed.). (2022). *Clinical handbook of psychological disorders: A step-by-step treatment manual* (6th ed.). New York, NY: The Guilford Press.

Barlow, D.H., Allen, L.B., & Choate, M.L. (2004). Toward a unified treatment for emotional disorders. *Behavior Therapy*, *35*, 205–230.

Becciu, M., & Colasanti, A.M. (2016). *Salute Mentale e Prevenzione*. Milano: Franco Angeli.

Beck, J.S. (2011). *Cognitive therapy: Basics and beyond* (2nd ed.). New York, NY: Guilford Press.

Boniwell, I. (2016). *Positive psychology: Theory, research and applications*. Oxford: McGraw-Hill.

Borgo, S., Sibilia, C., & Marks, I.M. (2015). *Dizionario clinico di psicoterapia. Una lingua comune*. Italia: Alpes.

Carcione, A., Niccolò, G., & Semerari, A. (2016). *Curare i casi complessi*. Bari-Roma: Laterza.

Cooper, M., & McLeod, J. (2011). Person-centered therapy: A pluralistic perspective. *Person-Centered and Experiential Psychotherapies, 10*(3), 210–223. doi:10.1080/147 79757.2011.599517

Davidson, D. (1987). *Subjective, intersubjective, objective*. Oxford: Oxford University Press.

Dell'Erba, G.L. (2008). *Diagnosi Psicologica*. Lecce: Pensa Editore.

Dell'Erba, G.L., & Nuzzo, E. (2010). *Psicologia Pratica*. Lecce: Pensa Editore.

Denman, C. (2001). Cognitive–analytic therapy. *Advances in Psychiatric Treatment, 7*(4), 243–252.

Diener, E. (1984). Subjective well-being. *Psychological Bulletin, 95*(3), 542–575.

Diener, E., & Diener, M. (1995). Cross-cultural correlates of life satisfaction and self-esteem. *Journal of Personality and Social Psychology, 68*(4), 653–663.

Diener, E., Lucas, R., & Scollon, C.N. (2006). Beyond the hedonic treadmill: Revising the adaptation theory of well-being. *American Psychologist, 61*(4), 305–314.

Dobson, K. (2010). *Handbook of cognitive behavior therapy*. New York, NY: Guilford Press.

Dobson, K.S., & Dozois, D.J.A. (2010). Historical and philosophical bases of the cognitive-behavioral therapies. In K.S. Dobson (Ed.), *Handbook of cognitive-behavior therapies* (3rd ed.). New York, NY: Guilford Press.

Gilbert, M., & Orlans, V. (2010). Technical eclecticism. In M. Gilbert & V. Orlans (Eds.), *Integrative therapy: 100 key points and techniques* (1st ed.). London: Routledge.

Hayes, S.C., & Hofmann, S.G. (2018). *Process based CBT*. Harbinger, Oakland: Content Press.

Hayes, S.C., Hofmann, S.G., & Ciarocchi, J. (2020). A process-based approach to psychological diagnosis and treatment: The conceptual and treatment utility of an extended evolutionary meta model. *Clinical Psychology Review, 82*, 101908.

Hayes, S.C., Strosahl, K.D., & Wilson, K.G. (2011). *Acceptance and commitment therapy: An experiential approach to behavior change*. New York, NY: Guilford Press.

James, W. (1950). *The principles of psychology* (Vols. 1 and 2); reprint of 1890 original. New York, NY: Dover.

Legrenzi, P. (2019). *Storia della psicologia* (6th ed.). Bologna: Il Mulino.

Legrenzi, P., & Umiltà, C. (2009). *Neuro mania. Il cervello non spiega chi siamo*. Bologna: Il Mulino.

Lemma, A., & Target, M. & Fonagy P. (2011). *Brief dynamic interpersonal therapy: A clinician's guide*. Oxford: Oxford University Press.

Luborsky, L., & Mark, D. (2015). Short-term supportive-expressive psychoanalytic psychotherapy. In P. Crits-Christoph & J. P. Barber (Eds.), *Handbook of short-term dynamic psychotherapy*. Chevy Chase, MD: International Psychotherapy Institute.

McCullough, J.P. Jr. (2000). *Treatment for chronic depression: Cognitive behavioral analysis system of pschotherapy (CBASP)*. New York, NY: Guilford Press.

Mancini, F., Mancini, A., & Castelfranchi, C. (2022). Unhealthy mind in A healthy body: A criticism to eliminativism in psychopathology. *Frontiers of Psychiatry, 13*, 889698.

McKay, M., Forsyth, J.P., & Eifert, G.H. (2010). *Your life on purpose: How to find what matters and create the life you want*. Oakland, CA: New Harbinger.

Mele, A. (2001). *Self-deception unmasked*. Princeton, NJ: Princeton University Press.

Miceli, M., & Castelfranchi, C. (2014). *Expectancy & emotions*. Oxford: Oxford University Press.

Norcross, J. (2012). *Psychotherapy relationship that work* (2nd ed.). New York, NY: American Psychological Association.

Norcross, J.C., & Goldfried, M.R. (2019). *Handbook of psychotherapy integration* (3rd ed.). New York, NY: Oxford University Press.

Robertson, D. (2019). *The philosophy of cognitive-behavioural therapy (CBT)*. London: Taylor and Francis.

Ryle, A. (1995). *Cognitive analytic therapy: Developments in theory and practice*. New York, NY: Wiley.

Sakaluk, J.K., Williams, A.J., Kilshaw, R.E., & Rhyner, K.T. (2019). Evaluating the evidential value of empirically supported psychological treatments (ESTs): A meta-scientific review. *Journal of Abnormal Psychology*, *128*(6), 500–509.

Stricker, G. (2001). An introduction to psychotherapy integration. *Psychiatric Times*, *18*(7).

Warburton, N. (2007). *Philosophy: The basics*. London: Routledge.

Weissman, A.N., & Beck, A.T., (1978, March). *Development and validation- of-the-dysfunctional attitude scale: A preliminary investigation*. Annual meeting of the American Educational Research Association.

Weissman, M.M., Markowitz, J.C., & Klerman, G.L. (2018). *The guide to interpersonal psychotherapy* (Updated and expanded edition). Oxford: Oxford University Press.

Young, J., Klosko, J.S., & Weishaar, M.E. (2003). *Schema therapy. A practitioner's guide*. New York, NY: Guilford Press.

Chapter 2

Processes and Contents

2.1 CBT Approach from Within

ABC-DE (Antecedents, Behaviours, Consequences, Disputation of Beliefs, and Evaluation), also known as a functional analysis, is generated from a plurality of perspectives, within Cognitive Behavioural Psychotherapy.

Albert Ellis developed the "ABC-DE" framework, which placed itself at the foundation of CBT. Aaron Beck subsequently developed a classic CBT intervention, the "Thought Record," based on Ellis and ABC's footsteps (Beck, 1975).

Functional analysis had already been utilised to evaluate behavioural consequences, which in themselves influenced behaviour (Skinner's Operant Conditioning) (Dobson, 2011; Skinner, 1975).

ABC is the epitome of cognitive psychology, as it places the meaning or the interpretation of individuals to determine their reactions, responses, or behaviours, at the core of psychological analysis. Our experiences could be organised or simplified, for the purpose to modify or intervene on specific events.

ABC has the following purposes and practical applications.

We can ask ourselves: what represents an Antecedent? By "A," we identify a stimulus, a fact, a situation, or a thought, which is the focus of our attention.

Usually, A is defined as the stimulus that activates or starts an event (an activating or triggering stimulus). For instance, a person who is greeting us, the phone ringing, a memory, or a sentence.

What is B – Behaviour? It is the evaluation, the interpretation, the judgement, or meaning, which we attribute to A.

B can be straightforward or elaborate; it does, however, convey meaning; it is congruous with a generic schema, which might denote a meaning loss, danger, fault, sense of direction, or physical proximity.

B plays a crucial role within functional analyses; however, it may be challenging to capture and to identify from an individual's perspective.

DOI: 10.4324/9781003299226-3

This is because it takes practice and requires introspective effort and reflection.

What is C – Consequences? It is the part that corresponds to emotional responses, feelings, and consequences of evaluation of B. Emotional responses can be several; the most common are fear, anxiety, sadness, depression, anger, shame, embarrassment, guilt, disgust, and humiliation.

With practice, an individual will be able to identify anxiety, anger, and sadness, as recurring emotions.

A – Stimulus – Event   B – Cognitions-Evaluations   C – Emotions

An example is illustrated as follows:

A: I am alone at home
B: No one cares about me
C: I feel depressed

2.2 ABC Can Be Complex

ABCs can be straightforward, but also extremely elaborate.

For instance, an event conceptualised as ABC may be straightforward (i.e. only one ABC), or complex (more than one ABC) to be evaluated in its entirety. A given stimulus, fact, or situation can be appraised in several ways and originate several parallel processes. Every ABC represents different "mental states," therefore different meanings, sometimes dichotomous in nature, i.e.

I am thinking about X	↔	I am thinking about X
B – I hate him	↔	B1 – I miss him
C – Anger	↔	C1 – Positive emotion

This is characteristic of fluctuating mental processes. An individual's perspective can be expressed by both ABCs.

ABCs can be represented as series or in a cascade connection. For instance,

A1 – Physical effort	→	B fear of becoming unwell	→	C anxiety
A2 – Anxiety	→	B2 worry that anxiety can cause a heart attack	→	C2 increased anxiety, and so forth in a vicious circle

I am scared of being anxious and therefore I am anxious.

It is important to emphasise that, instead of reflecting and identifying why we experience certain emotions and awareness of "mind in place," we focus on emotions themselves as if they were further problems, thus generating vicious cycles and psychological traps. Such stance generates secondary problems stemming from primary problems:

| Situation | $\rightarrow$ | B – Interpretation | $\rightarrow$ | C – Emotion |
| A2 – Emotional State | $\rightarrow$ | B2 – Evaluation | $\rightarrow$ | C2 – Emotion |

In summary, ABC can be straightforward or complex and offers conceptualisation of vicious circles. We have a propensity to focus on our mental processes and emotional consequences, rather than on the reliability of our judgement, thus building psychological traps.

2.3 Evaluation of B

Our Bs could represent a conceptualisation of our insight as "seizing our inner dialogue."

We usually experience ongoing inner dialogues with ourselves, as Socrates stated, and as mentioned by Plato and Antisthenes. This reflects the most important aspect of our experience and is linked to the way in which we evaluate our own selves, in relation to ourselves and to our interpersonal world (Robertson, 2019).

A dialogue within us is always active: this is also a crucial process in children's psychological development. These internal dialogues are almost always automatic, and subconscious.

It is crucial to experience a temporary pause, a sort of internal gaze within our own mind. We capture fragments of sentences, or automatic thoughts, or expressions such as "whatever, there we go, there it is, damn..." We can only subsequently identify specific evaluations and cognitions.

2.4 Thought Content

Dialogic and verbal features of cognitive content can be categorised as follows:

* Hypotheses or inferences
* Judgement and evaluations

Hypotheses and inferences are attempts to predict future events and anticipate what might happen. They are affirmations with a question mark in the end. Individuals do not know what will happen, but they behave as they already know. Individuals may not be aware that they are formulating hypotheses rather than facts (Beck, 1975).

Judgements and evaluation are thoughts and affirmations characterised by positive or negative connotations: they can express desire, preferences, pretences, principles experienced by the individual, or personal views on the world or human beings. For instance, "I agree with this person," "I like this or that," or "I prefer doing this, rather than something else."

At this stage, there is no context built on facts, but only the individuals' preferences and choices. This is where we are in everlasting dialogue with ourselves. With practice or psychotherapy, we may capture snapshots of this dialogue and intervene directly on the hypotheses or unjustified and unhelpful affirmations (Beck, 2011).

This kind of internal dialogue is characterised by hypotheses and evaluations. Within such internal dialogue, we may discern how we think about ourselves. Such a sense of self is always in relation to other individuals and to our interpersonal world.

Sense of self may be explored with our patients or clients by asking, "what would this mean to you?" or "what would this say about you?" This is an effective way to support a person to connect such thoughts with deeper aspects of unhelpful cognitions and beliefs, such as dysfunctional assumptions and negative schema (Beck, 2011).

Hypotheses and evaluations are traditionally addressed and treated with Cognitive Restructuring Techniques and its different variants. Hypothesis testing and evaluation through identification of triggers, with links to personal history, has the intent to create a change in perspective, with regard to both contents and relationship that individuals have with their own psychological functioning, i.e. metacognition, self-distancing, and Theory of Mind.

Furthermore, our own sense of self but also relationships with others and our interpersonal world are often generic and excessively condensed: whilst they capture the most salient aspects of ourselves, or at least the aspects towards which we are most attuned, they leave all of other perspectives out.

Our sense of self, defined as personal or cognitive schema, is characterised by biases and patterns (Beck, 2011) and operates as such: Schemas' modification requires strenuous efforts without consistent practice and psychotherapy. Moreover, personal Schemas filter subjective experiences. Cognitive psychologists derived this concept from Immanuel Kant's Critique of Pure Reason (Legrenzi, 2019); Kant expanded and reappraised Stoicism as a foundation of his Critique.

Let us focus on Schemas (Beck, 2011; Legrenzi, 2019).

When an individual perceives himself as vulnerable, he might feel the world around him as dangerous, and his health as uncertain.

Another person might believe she is a failure, and perceives others as excessively intransigent, and the world as a constant source of problems.

A man may believe to be vulnerable, or helpless, and potentially a victim; he might perceive others as potential abusers, and the world as a place filled with dangers and life full of humiliation.

These are just a few examples of individuals that experience others and the world in which they live, filtered by their own personal Schemas, own ideas, and act with persistent biases.

Is it plausible to wonder what kind of typological classification may be utilised to categorise such Schemas?

This depends on several factors: psychologists or psychiatrists refer to Schemas for clinical purposes, in relation to clinical research and empirical data.

For instance, Beck (2011) defined Schemas as structures for screening, coding, and evaluating stimuli that impinge on the mind. Based on Schemas, individuals are able to categorise and interpret their experiences in a meaningful way.

Jeffrey Young (Young, Klosko, & Weishaar, 2003), Beck's former student, devised a list that is divided between 11 and 18 Schemas, grouped in five domains:

1 Disconnection and Rejection
2 Impaired Autonomy and Performance
3 Impaired Limits
4 Other-Directedness
5 Over Vigilance and Inhibition

For instance, in an 11-format schema, we may find some Schemas that are concerned with different appraisal and aspects of life. Such Schemas are as follows:

- Abandonment
- Mistrust/Abuse
- Emotional Deprivation
- Social Isolation/Alienation
- Vulnerability to Harm or Illness
- Enmeshment/Undeveloped Self
- Failure
- Unrelenting Standards
- Entitlement/Grandiosity

Often maladaptive Schemas may coexist creating a damaging sense of selves; this often occurs in relation to our own early experiences and events where our own Schemas originated (Young et al., 2003).

For instance, fear of abandonment (abandonment schema) may lead to fear of failure, which might result in development of beliefs of unrelenting standards.

These beliefs illustrate the evolution of the individual's self-focus and clarify why he thinks about himself in a certain way, based on his early experiences and story.

Cognitive Schemas not only are characterised by stereotypical content, but they also filter reality and direct experience of human beings.

When examining the self-affirmations typical of each one of the eleven cognitive Schemas identified by Young, we notice in what way such assumptions play a key role in "filtering" cognitions and building psychological traps.

The alternative is to identify them on the basis of their true nature of inflexible and repetitive rules, which filters the individual experience and which individuals might have about his own context and environment.

To cite Jeffrey Young (Young et al., 2003), Schemas can be summarised as follows:

- Please don't leave me (I beg you not to leave me) – Abandonment
- I do not trust you – Mistrust and Abuse
- I will never be loved/I will never receive the love I need – Emotional Deprivation
- I cannot fit in – Social Isolation/Alienation
- Something terrible is going to happen soon – Vulnerability to Harm and Illness
- I am a worthless – Undeveloped Self
- I am a failure – Failure
- I will do whatever you want me to do – Subjugation
- Nothing is ever good enough – Unrelenting Standards
- I can have whatever I want – Entitlement/Grandiosity

We all have our own ideas as to our own sense of self; however, some individuals' beliefs are generic, absolute, and negative; in this case, these Schemas act like biases and filter experience.

Schemas may be single or complex and are always interconnected; this aspect might be challenging to identify throughout the exploration of early experiences.

Furthermore, Schemas are specific to individuals and attempt to categorise them based on a standard list, which may lead to oversimplification.

An alternative way to identify Schemas is to identify a life theme, which provides a broader perspective, as it leads to development coping strategies to address negative self-belief.

We will explore this notion in the next chapters.

2.5 Emotions

Emotions could be shaped by the meaning that we attribute to internal and external events and stimuli (Beck, 2011).

Meaning is often in relation to our sense of self or Schemas. It can be meaningful for the person who undergoes psychotherapy to discover the beliefs underlying the schema. When considering ABC, for instance, an Antecedent may generate a Behaviour linked to danger and threat, which in turn might generate a Consequence linked to Anxiety.

A "B" related to fault might generate an emotion linked to Anger. Lastly, when we attribute a meaning of loss to an Antecedent, we might experience Sadness as a Consequence.

Although emotional reactions and responses or the attribution given to feelings may be complex and are at the core of an ongoing debate in psychological research, we may refer to three core emotions that are at the centre of human struggles: Anger, Sadness, and Anxiety.

The difference between emotions, mood, and feelings may generate confusion.

It is therefore crucial to develop a befitting lexicon concerning emotions and feelings (Legrenzi, 2019).

Emotions are the responses that we attribute to events.

Emotions are transient in nature, whereas feelings have longer duration and added complexity (Legrenzi, 2019): both, however, are used interchangeably in psychological practice.

The term Mood is used to provide an approximation of emotional states, in order to establish if our mood is low or elevated, positive or negative. The term "Frame of Mind" is synonymous with Emotion and Feeling; its roots are literary, rather than psychological in nature.

Emotions are generated from meaning attributed to and evaluations stemming from events.

Meanings are linked to each goal, and emotions are reactions to representations that individuals give to such intents.

Thus, the term "Emotions" has several synonyms, i.e. Feelings or Mood.

In our work, we refer to emotional states, namely as "emotions" or "feelings." The difference between Mood, Feelings, and Emotions is not relevant in the contexts explored within this book, as it is mostly obsolete and a by-product of cultural and literary variations.

Emotions are transient and depend on the meaning and attributions given by each individual. Emotions are reactions that depend on each individual's evaluation on specific core goals (Legrenzi, 2019; Miceli & Castelfranchi, 2014).

However, there is more.

As may be gathered from their etymological meaning, emotions are states of our being that result in being compelled to act or react.

Depending on the meaning or the evaluation of a given antecedent, the subsequent emotion not only represents feelings, but also an action in keeping with the evaluation given by the individual. Emotions are deeply linked to our propensity to act; however, this may not correspond to an action within an observable behaviour. Our physiological systems in action (i.e. Bio-Behavioral; Panksepp & Davis, 2018) might be linked with this concept.

For instance, a student who is about to sit an exam and believes that a negative outcome is more likely experiences anxiety and tension and feels inclined not to attend the exam (avoidance) or is likely to consistently experience rumination and worry.

If a person left by his partner attributes a sense of significant loss to this event, he might feel despondent and compelled to be disengaged and apathetic, whilst imagining future scenarios linked to such loss. In this case, we refer to worry, rather than rumination. Rumination is linked to the past; worry is linked to the future.

A further example is an individual who is the victim of theft; he might evaluate this as injustice and feeling wronged. He might experience anger (aggressive reaction) and be compelled to react and repair such injustice by exacting revenge. He might be therefore likely to focus on future scenarios focused on injustice (aggressive worry).

In summary, emotions are complex constructs that stem from the meaning of our evaluations. They are characterised by neurobiological components, behavioural reactions, or "need/push for action" (Dobson, 2010).

Emotions are states of living organisms; the result of natural selection of mammals and slowly evolved to complex states in relation to different parts of the brain, and their interaction with physical and relational environments over 500,000 years.

Emotions are states reactive to meaning that we attribute to events: they have a neurobiological and action-driven component that is specific and coordinated within themselves.

To conclude, emotions are states of living organisms, and the result of mammal evolution in order to ensure survival.

2.6 Internal Dialogue

Anything that lies within our internal dialogue is part of the evaluation of our thought processes, which are constantly operative within ourselves. These cognitions represent important signals of automatic activity, which we would be unable to identify, given the extensive amount of information that our brain processes simultaneously (Legrenzi, 2019).

These cognitions are defined by Beck (1975, 2011) as "Automatic Thoughts." Automatic thoughts may be useful to individuals who undergo psychotherapy, when we attempt to identify the meaning associated with an event, or an emotion. This can be done in several ways, by

- Asking ourselves for instance "what was I thinking at that moment in time" or "what was going through my mind when I was feeling anxious" allows access to our internal dialogue, to our ongoing and incessant thought process, through language
- Formulate questions such as "what does this mean?" As a consequence, a person can therefore identify the meaning of his mental states, understand himself better, make sense of the situation, and understand why he feels a certain way. This is a specific intervention that occurs in cognitive psychotherapy
- We might be curious: what is the meaning of this intervention? When a person asks himself, "what does this mean?" he attempts to identify an automatic thought. The meaning that is sought is related to an event, a stimulus, or a belief that has been expressed in relation to a certain situation and evaluated as such. This question may help to identify our own personal rules or behaviours and to decode certain situations

Possible meanings generally lead to three different categories of evaluations (Beck, 2011):

1 Automatic Thoughts
2 Dysfunctional Beliefs or Assumptions (Catastrophising, Overgeneralisation, and Personalising)
3 Schemas or Core Beliefs (Abandonment, Failure, etc.)

Such categories can be steadily and thoroughly processed by a person, from the first to the last: Schemas or core beliefs are the most challenging to identify.

Automatic thoughts are part of our mental activity; they reflect our internal appraisals immediately and directly and are easily accessible. Those thoughts may usually be identified by the questions "what am I thinking just now?" or "what was I thinking at a given moment?" Automatic Thoughts usually reflect the meaning of Dysfunctional Beliefs and Schemas.

Dysfunctional Beliefs or Assumptions are intermediate cognitive modalities. They are characterised by rigid rules, arbitrary inferences, and notably polarised opinions; they represent the application of Schemas to everyday situations and life.

Schemas or Core Beliefs epitomise meanings that individuals shape on themselves, and their own future. Schemas are not immediately accessible but may be discovered and addressed through psychotherapeutic interventions. They are intrinsic to individuals' emotional and social development and stem from early life experiences.

Beck's Theory argues that Automatic Thoughts and Dysfunctional Assumptions are generated and influenced by Cognitive Schemas (Beck 1975, 2011). This is in line with the current perspectives in CBT; cognitive Schemas are considered essential factors in psychological functioning.

Much can be said about B.

We may ask ourselves as to whether our thought processes are accurate; nonetheless it would be equally as important to reflect in what way we interpreted a situation related to B.

We will consider how there is a core "duality" within ourselves: one concerning a stimulus, or a problem; the other concerning the individual himself allows the individual to "calibrate" himself and to tone down the inevitable errors of his own mind.

Engaging within our own inner dialogue means to be willing to reflect upon ourselves and to focus on multiple thoughts that we experience continuously. Initially we may discover evaluations of threat, loss, or blame. These are likely to be associated with emotions, experienced as anxiety, sadness, or anger.

Recognition of a given emotion leads to discernment of meaning. Emotional states can be very different from each other and categorised through contextual adjectives, names, or situations (Alford & Beck, 1997). Nevertheless, it may suffice to become skilled at identifying our core emotions (joy, fear, sadness, anger, and disgust) and other re-occurring ones (shame, envy, embarrassment, fault, and boredom).

Focusing on an inner dialogue also means discerning between emotions and their appraisals, starting from a generic meaning, which becomes increasingly complex.

This focus relies on a person's ability to identify his own emotions and link B to C or, vice versa, C to B. This can be practised in CBT. The main point is to "identify the meaning and function of B."

Self-improvement and taking control of the life we wish to live requires knowing ourselves; this might entail the ability to discern and differentiate our internal thought processes or improve our own metacognitions.

Within our inner dialogue's incessant activity, there are three different kinds of appraisal of events (Alford & Beck, 1997).

The first kind is generic and is concerned with desire, danger, loss, and blame.

The second is complex and is concerned with processing and evaluating information in relation to events; it may be categorised in six groups. Such cognitive activity is sophisticated and yet fast and automatic in nature. A person may not always be aware of his interpretation of reality and events, but he might become aware of it when the focus of his attention is within, rather than out with himself.

Information processing can be categorised as follows (Beck, 2011):

- Overgeneralising – characterised by the inability to discern between an event and its context, and seeing a pattern based on such an event, thus drawing broad conclusions
- Catastrophising – dwelling on extreme negative scenarios and predicting the worst possible outcome, thus exaggerating the likelihood of their occurrence
- Egocentrism-mental filter – perceiving the world from our own perspective, without considering or evaluating other people's perspective or the broader context. Whatever is in our mind morphs into what we perceive might happen
- Distress intolerance – the belief that any situation may be stressful or challenging and that this event will be too painful and impossible to tolerate. This is concerned with the belief that an individual cannot tolerate distress and therefore may be hypersensitive towards any kind of stress
- Labelling – when a person is critical towards others, thus shifting responsibility to other individuals for his own actions
- Self-Criticism – when a person blames himself for events or situations that are not his own responsibility. At the foundation of this thinking error, there is a bias towards us, and our own beliefs on our own worth as individuals

2.7 How to Reflect on Our Own B

This process is referred to in the literature as metacognition (Hayes & Hofmann, 2018). We will identify and reflect on these important features of behaviour, whether they are hypotheses or core beliefs. We may formulate a hypothesis in relation to an observable experience.

It might be helpful to consider hypotheses that are characterised by a negative outcome (i.e. catastrophic scenarios and perceived inability to cope with such events), so that we may utilise a cognitive framework to determine if there are facts that support predicted negative outcomes.

We may ask ourselves if we "can predict the future" and what kind of evidence we have to foresee any events. Imagination is different from knowledge, and it is important to consider this. It is important to reformulate hypotheses, a catastrophic one, and a realistic alternative, for instance, so that we may determine what facts are stemming from these premises; a chain of facts can hardly be disputed.

This may only occur if events are formulated as inferences or hypotheses (Beck, 2011) i.e. X will happen, I will therefore suffer Y, and the situation will become Z.

Core beliefs, or Schemas, are conceptualised differently (Young et al., 2003). They are extreme and based on our own egocentric beliefs and disconnected from everyone else's perspectives. Schemas do not offer any other alternative perspectives for our consideration, when we feel differently, and we are part of a diverse context. These evaluations should be considered within a commensurate, proportionate context. It is vital that a person acknowledges he might have adopted a polarised stance (black or white thinking). Attempting to identify a middle path, even if just theoretically, becomes an effective intervention. This intervention achieves its purpose when a person develops his realistic, rather than schema-driven, alternative. To conclude, this work can support increased awareness, which results in minimising the occurrence of polarisation of judgement from one perspective only.

The content, for instance, indicates an individual's own interests whilst Schemas represent areas of meaning for the individuals. A way to consider an inflexible rule (Beck, 2011) is to identify rules or dysfunctional assumptions, as contents. Contents may be infinite, but all it matters is that in the end they are summarised in recurring themes: they are defined as conditional beliefs (Beck, 2011).

There are beliefs that morph into conditional beliefs, i.e. if X happens, therefore a condition that means Y also exists. Such dysfunctional assumptions are based on the prerequisite that an individual becomes bonded to them, as if they were "rules."

Psychologists have identified a list of dysfunctional beliefs that also led to the development of scales, such as the Dysfunctional Attitude Scale – DAS (Weissman & Beck, 1978). These are categorised as follows:

- Validation
- Affective Dependency
- Success
- Perfectionism
- Entitlement
- Grandiosity/Omnipotence
- Insufficient Self-Control

Such dysfunctional assumptions contribute towards a negative functioning of the individual and are indicators of directions towards individuals' values.

However, individuals tend to direct their efforts to achieve their goals through these assumptions: they therefore turn into obstacles towards living a meaningful life.

Each one of these factors maintains, although indirectly, a conditional limit to his or her own personal value (Dell'Erba & Nuzzo, 2010; Ellis, 1964). For instance, in relationships, when affirming the need for love, individuals feel that if he is not loved, he is worth nothing as a person. In the need for success, an individual may state that if he does not succeed or if he is not at the top of a certain field, he is worth nothing.

Need for validation – identifies the inflexible belief that an individual sets for himself. "If people do not approve of me, or like me, then everything will go wrong and I am worth nothing."

Affective dependency – focuses on the rule whereby individuals feel they are worthless; unless they are loved by a significant other, they generally consider themselves unlovable, when this is not the case

Need for success – identifies the need to be successful and achieve goals; otherwise individuals consider themselves to be worthless

Perfectionism – when individuals gauge their worth on the need not to make mistakes and focus on perfection and unrelenting standards; otherwise they consider themselves worthless

Entitlement – when individuals act and extend their own responsibility towards issues which are out of their control, thus putting their own self-worth at risk if or when this is not achieved

Insufficient self-control – it is characterised by beliefs related to not having any control over ourselves. This identifies a superficial, passive stance, which results in putting at risk our own sense of worth

These beliefs cover crucial grounds for individuals and provide additional information on what is important, provided that they are placed within a balanced perspective. They represent rules that lead the subject towards a certain sense of direction towards what is really important to him and what kind of person he aspires to be (Burn, 1980).

Identification of these kinds of cognitions and beliefs is a meaningful therapeutic work and helps to identify a part of our mind that reminds us what matters to us, and what we place as a hurdle. Furthermore, this work supports the comprehension of our mind, and how we function: it has its own value.

2.8 The Mind and the Knowledge of the Self

Human mind is complex. A total of 1000 pages would be insufficient to identify with reasonable precision all of its functions and aspects. Can we categorise groups of functions and abilities to create a synthesis of the human mind?

An oversimplification leads us to consider an initial part of the mind as an archive of knowledge and information (Dell'Erba et al., 2009; Legrenzi, 2019). This part organises knowledge (i.e. the information that is related to our external world and ourselves as part of the same); another part organises past events, concerned with memories that we experience in the first instance. Obviously, there is not an obvious distinction between these categories, as they complement each other. Other information or what we know is concerned with who we are as an object of our own knowledge.

Another part of the mind is characterised by conscious or semi-conscious aspects and voluntary or semi-voluntary aspects, such as reasoning, evaluation, judgement, interpretation, and problem-solving (Dell'Erba et al., 2009).

The crucial aspect of this part is that we "live" within it. We talk, we think, and we determine our actions starting from this "being" in such mind mode; we can feel more about who we are than what we remember.

A third part is characterised by a hardly voluntary part: this is called imagination, or ideation, or intrusive thoughts (Dell'Erba et al., 2009; Wells, 1997). These activities, with some differences within them, have the purpose of creating virtual scenarios with the aim to foresee, to confront events, and to survive.

It may happen to negatively evaluate some imaginative aspects or intrusive thoughts and try in different ways not to experience them. This leads to impossible attempts to eradicate these thoughts, and their negative evaluation. It is the attempt to eliminate these thoughts that result in making intrusive, involuntary thoughts more repetitive. This process becomes paradoxical in nature, whereas it is by giving ourselves the freedom to think freely that normalises these thoughts. Freud would say that we might diminish and alleviate our own censorship (Legrenzi, 2019).

Understanding our own mind, even at the most basic level, allows us to improve ourselves and to achieve self-determination. Conversely, an incorrect theory of our own mental processes may deprive us of opportunities and action on ourselves and our world. Furthermore, an incorrect understanding of our mind may lead to impossible pursuits, such as not to think and not to feel emotions.

A generic but correct theory is a prerequisite of good functioning. This intervention is called psychoeducation (Farrand, 2020): information about psychological processes with the purpose of improving our beliefs and information of our mind and psychology in general, that is.

Psychoeducation as intervention adds to a general view of ourselves as human beings. Although psychology is not concerned with such broad theoretical aspects, it is crucial to perceive ourselves as human beings. This is because a general idea serves as an orientation in multiple specific sectors and may add a sense of purpose and motivation to our actions, projects, and will to live.

A useful albeit reductive way to do this is to consider some aspects within a synchronic perspective, and others within a diachronic perspective (i.e. some aspects can be considered within a present, past, and future timeline) (Hayes, Strosahal, & Wilson, 2012).

A synchronic perspective represents a complex way of thinking about ourselves; it is characterised by several aspects of ourselves as human beings. This leads to a better understanding of our own mind, such as learning to comprehend our own mind and be cognisant of its processes. It also helps us to reflect on our bound by the laws with Nature, as everything in our planet, and trust our ability to develop meaningful goals and aims, based on a valued sense of direction. A synchronic perspective can help to differentiate between the following:

- Cognitive, self-reflective, self-knowledge, and self-improvement area, concerning being sufficiently expert of our own minds, and aware of our own perspectives
- An area related to our being in this world, as a part of this world and subject to its laws, but also being able to observe the world around us without any biases or reactions
- An area related to the meaning and choices that underpin our actions, and our behaviours towards others, with their goals and feelings, even in relation to values that inform our actions and what is good to us – we will focus on this synchronous perspective later on

Differently, a diachronic perspective is a way of bearing in mind, over time, where our attention is directed, and how we think about ourselves and in relation to our goals or aims in the past, present, or future. In what context we are, or we think we are, and where we position our goals: this is a fundamental question posed by a diachronic perspective. A diachronic perspective is focused on a timeline:

- In the past – the beliefs that concern us and the events from which biases stemmed from challenging thoughts, or a certain belief about ourselves, or simply finding a sense of our own biography
- In the present – what facilitates and what gets in the way of our commitment and involvement in the world, along with being able to find it and our willingness to become involved with what surrounds us
- In the future – it is relevant to determine what our goals, projects, and aims that interest us are and that are possible to achieve, the paths that we want to walk on and that really matter to us

Our aim is to practise, in order to improve ourselves. In psychotherapy, it may be useful to reflect on such schema or whole view of the world, in order to tease apart difficulties.

Equally, we may utilise this view to identify our strengths. If we imagine two orthogonal axes, i.e. the horizontal is from Past to Future and the vertical axis from the Physical to our Psychological world, we may identify the intersection in the here and now and that can represent the perspective from which we evaluate ourselves.

2.9 The Self-Esteem Conundrum and Sense of Self

The self-esteem conundrum starts when we think about ourselves, our way to self-evaluate ourselves or criticise ourselves (Dell'Erba & Nuzzo, 2010; Ellis, 1964).

Self-esteem and self-efficacy are widely, albeit ostensibly, used concepts; this might pose a potential concern to evaluate or to self-attribute a value to us (Dell'Erba & Nuzzo, 2010).

Self-esteem is a generic and ambiguous term. It is concerned with the worth that an individual has towards himself, and based on how we think about ourselves and our measure of such worth based on how people evaluate our performance (Ellis, 1964).

Self-efficacy is a construct concerned with the belief in our ability to engage in behaviours that result in attaining goals. It also reflects the ability to take control and responsibility for our behaviours (Bandura, 1977). Self-evaluation may be a very complex, hazardous, and disputable process. Let's focus on two different ways of self-evaluating ourselves.

- As a person and
- As a whole consisting of several sides (therefore one or more aspects)

Self-evaluation as a person in relation to a specific context may be useful, as it can lead to self-improvement, provided that such specific context is relevant, and meaningful.

We constructively evaluate ourselves as individuals; this appraisal leads to change, focus, and acceptance of our limitations. We can also accept others' appraisals, given that they might provide useful feedback and can be added to our own personal perspective; those opinions can be ignored if irrelevant.

An individual may present with several relevant contexts within his life: a balance characterised by commitment and esteem, resources to improve ourselves, and be ready to accept our limitations as imperfect and fallible human beings.

Often a limitation or a poor performance in a certain context may be linked to a good outcome in a different context.

We all have our preferences, our interests, and our favourite areas within our preferences. However, it may be hazardous if damaging, to operate our own self-evaluation as persons, focussing on our areas of interests, performances, and practical aspects. An evaluation of our worth based on our abilities or capabilities is a perilous stance, for instance, "I am a failure," rather than "I failed in X or Y" (Ellis, 1964).

Even if individuals perform poorly in their own areas of interest, they are still individuals like all of us. We may conceptualise Self-Worth, as very similar to the concept of Dignity (Warburton, 2007). Our Self- Worth as individuals should not be evaluated either by ourselves or by other people; this is not possible, not even if the person wanted to do so.

In fact, where would anyone find "measures" to define human qualities? Those measures do not and cannot exist. In this instance, it is essential to reflect that the concept of Self-Esteem may be used and reserved to a specific area, as Self-Worth, and never as a general idea.

No one can persuade or prove that differences in wealth, sports performances, mathematical abilities, and successful careers may identify or generate Self-Worth (Dell'Erba & Nuzzo, 2010; Ellis, 1964). Some individuals may be anxious or depressed, due to their personal belief that their own Self-Worth is generated by success or validation in specific areas. Nevertheless, it is crucial to empower individuals to be curious about the surrounding world or any other areas that might become an interest. Narrow interests lead to access to new information and decreased involvement in what surrounds people.

Whilst Self-Worth may not be evaluated or measured whilst Self-Efficacy may be, it is convenient to do so. In fact it is useful to receive feedback, provided that we wish to receive it and accept it.

Any system equipped with goals and drive requires new information to grow, to interface, and interact with different environments and individuals. In a similar fashion, individuals may look for new information, new goals, thus developing new capabilities; this will lead or might contribute to lead, to interact, and interface with more context, or simply different environments that require different capabilities or ways of adapting, thus increasing coping and flexibility to adapt. Conversely, a closed system may not flexibly adapt and may only survive in stationary environments. Individuals with little interests and goals do not fulfil their potential, whilst their ability to adapt becomes circumscribed. Furthermore, our own interests are aims and goals pursued, or being pursued, through self-efficacy; this results in involved and rewarded Flow Experience and tends to broaden our capabilities' range and opportunities to flourish (i.e. Seligman and Fredrickson, the Broaden and Building Theory) (Boniwell, 2016).

2.10 Locus of Control

Our locus of control (LoC) is crucial, but control might become a problem.

What are we trying to control? Why do we try to control? What is the desired outcome of control? What are the undesirable outcomes of control? To what extent do we have the ability to control what is around us? Is this an inadvertent automatic need, or does it constitute a motivation driven by individuals?

Epictetus provided us with meaningful considerations in this regard. In the Enchiridion, Epictetus formulated the following concept:

Of things that exist, some are in our power and some are not in our power. Those that are in our power are conception, choice, desire, aversion, and in a word, those things that are our own doing. Those that are not under our control are the body, property or possessions, reputation, positions of authority, and in a word, such things that are not our own doing.

Control is often aimed at managing a threat, which might impact on something we cannot live or do without.

What is so crucial and indefeasible? It might be our Self-Worth. Although individuals identify their existence as human beings as essential, Self-Worth represents the dignity of existence. Our Self-Worth does not get lost and is not threatened as is attributed to our existence. However, although this concept is almost taken for granted, as an ideological perspective of us as human beings, it is part of the World Health Organization (WHO) of Human Rights.

Self-Worth is a perspective of human beings. In fact, we can all think of some tragic alternatives present in Humankind, i.e. Nazism, Deviation from Communist Ideologies, Sects, and one-dimensional derivatives of Capitalism, that are void of Self-Worth. Self-Worth is the psychological equivalent of the concept of Life and Living Being in Bioethics. What is worth, what represents worth? The concept of unconditional Self-Worth is opposed to a Specific Worth and own efficacy, which covers aspects of judgements concerning others and ourselves (Dell'Erba & Nuzzo, 2010; Ellis, 1964).

Thus, LoC is not something good in itself and the opposite is not bad. LoC is part of our own boundaries as human beings; it establishes what is within our power and what is not, i.e. what is out with our control or influence. We may attempt to establish what is and what is not within our control; whenever we engage in this process, we discover that several activities, even within ourselves, are not within our power. This means that any attempt to establish an internal LoC of anything which is not intentional is destined to fail. What is the level of control that we have as individuals in relation to what is within our power and what is not (Epictetus, 1865; Robertson, 2019)? In what way can we relate ourselves to what is not within our internal LoC? With strong reactions? With stronger control? Avoiding, or attempting to alter outcomes? All of this seems in vain and counterproductive. How can we appraise or reappraise what is not within our control or is unintentional?

This perspective encourages us to widen our ideas, actions, and experiences. Conscience, Choice, and Meaning seem to be philosophical terms from at least a century ago. However, they are currently utilised to contribute to modern psychological therapies.

It is worth considering that what might cause suffering is to set goals that are not within our LoC. This results in frustration that cannot be justified. When we ask ourselves why we might not be able to find a justification for what happens, we might end up in a sort of argument with the Gods, to cite Stoic philosophers.

It reminds us of the Story of the Archer (Robertson, 2019). The Archer pulled back the bow and shot the arrow, trying his best to hit the target. The Archer aimed and shot the arrow with as much care and attention as possible. Hitting the target was not in the Archer's power. A sudden wind might have blown, for instance. Such event would be external to the Archer's LoC. However, the Archer knew that his happiness did not depend on whether the arrow reached the right spot.

This is a powerful metaphor of LoC by Cicero.

Sometimes we try to control, avoid, eliminate, or modify our emotions, our unhelpful thoughts, and physical sensations associated with them, which may be considered a paradoxical process: the more you do it, the more you have them.

In this instance, we all experience being stuck and trapped within these processes. The more we try to control, the more we are trapped by them and the more we are stuck and cannot move backwards or forwards. Most importantly, we may not head towards our chosen sense of direction.

The problem is not the presence of an intrusive thought, or a negative emotion, but the way in which we respond to them, or we attempt to extend our LoC to them and on such subjective emotions (Dobson, 2010; Miceli & Castelfranchi, 2014).

It is important to acknowledge what we can and cannot control, in order to change our behaviour.

There are alternative options when attempting to create a LoC on what we cannot control; for example attempting to create an internal LoC, when the situation in fact is not within our control; this approach generally fails.

Thoughts or emotions, beliefs, or memories may take up the function of negative stimuli, hazardous in nature, not sustainable, thus aversive and deemed to be avoided or suppressed.

The tendency to negatively appraise our difficult emotions as dangerous, or events to avoid or suppress, is generated by and throughout a long learning process. This process might be affected by social rules on what is right and what is wrong and should be avoided.

2.11 Complex Emotions

Complex emotions are often concerned with social aspects of our lives; they might represent our frames of mind, which are determined by social purposes or related to social and interpersonal roles (Miceli & Castelfranchi, 2014).

For instance, guilt and shame.

Social emotions are inherent to individuals involved in self-appraisals, or appraisals of others towards us and us towards others.

Guilt could be a "pang" stemming from social conscience (remorse) or an acute, lived experience of guilt.

Individuals evaluate some aspects of their own guilt, albeit unconsciously (Miceli & Castelfranchi, 2014). These aspects are

- Presence of a sufferer towards whom we feel guilty
- Presence of an unjustified damage, in which we feel involved
- Perceived direct and intentional responsibility, towards a certain event

For instance, two students are studying for the same exam. However, one of them passes and the other one fails. The student who passed felt guilty. In-depth exploration indicates that the student who passes feels he has a bond with the student who fails, and who is "unlucky."

On other occasions, for instance, we feel guilty despite the absence of sufferers, i.e. an individual is going through a red light and feels guilty even if there is no one around. What emerges in this instance is that such individuals feel they have committed a transgression, which has theoretically put others at disadvantage or in danger, despite the fact that nothing happened.

Guilt can be "moral" when it is in relation to doing "bad versus good," but with emphasis on personal responsibility (Miceli & Castelfranchi, 2014). Guilt can be deontological or Kantian when an event occurs in relation to a deontological code, in which case bad is represented by committing the offence per se (D'Olimpo & Mancini, 2014; Warburton, 2007).

There is a third possibility, whereby a person experiences guilt as the mere thought of having hurt or offended another person, without anyone informing the individual about this (Paternalistic guilt). To intervene on these frames of mind is essential to reframe core beliefs pertinent to these three different experiences in which the person was involved.

Shame is the emotion concerning the belief that individuals are criticised by others who are important and have a meaningful role in the individual's life.

Shame implies a social judgement, i.e. reputation. Reputation stems from a social necessity and is concerned with having information pertinent to the conduct and reliability of an individual. Clearly this information may be vague, distorted, or hasty and not directly verifiable. Shame is the direct result of these processes.

We react to the threat posed to their reputation. If and when we are interpersonally sensitive, we cannot face these circumstances or be seen; this can lead to considering that we have our own Schemas and believe that others have the same negative tendencies.

Being able to experience shame means, within certain limits, that we adhere to social rules; to be void of sense of shame is a negative indicator, i.e. being without scruples.

Each emotion might be linked to a negative self-evaluation, whenever this is experienced or not, for instance, "I feel ashamed as I am experiencing tangible shame."

Embarrassment is often wrongly mistaken for Shame.

We might experience embarrassment when we struggle to evaluate certain kinds of social rules in public and the necessity to have information as to how to behave in certain circumstances.

For instance, how we behave in the lift, or when we are invited in an unfamiliar household. In these contexts, we seek points of reference to conform and adapt.

When we experience embarrassment, we seem to lack information as to how to behave in public places, and social skills. Psychologists often consider social skills as an end in relation to the lack of individuals' social skills.

Then we have **Envy,** a controversial emotion.

Envy might be a problematic social emotion as it is often kept secret; it is rarely accepted as a legitimate feeling.

We may envy individuals if they have something that we do not possess, which we would like to have but don't. We might feel that such individuals are undeserving of what they have, and thus we perceive this as unjust. An envious person may experience malevolent feelings and wish misfortune to other individuals, rather than admiration (if he recognises the merit), or happiness (due to benevolent predisposition), or sorrow (thus focusing attention on the person's difficulties).

This kind of self-evaluation has its foundation, albeit not on intentional grounds, on a discrepancy of what we possess or have in relation to another individual, resulting in apparent missing equity and equality. Envy is hard to express, due to their own implicit admission of inferiority and malevolent feelings. Envy flourishes when there is a critical attachment to wealth linked to social status and appearances.

2.12 Case Example

Maria was a 20-year-old university student in economics, the only child of two parents, who worked as an administrative clerk.

Maria was assessed by a psychiatrist in a community mental health setting, initially for a suspected restrictive eating disorder. Maria was referred to one of the authors, EN, for further diagnostic assessment, formulation, and psychotherapeutic intervention.

Maria was administered a SCID-P test, and a further assessment identified an anxiety disorder, with Specific Phobia, Panic Disorder, and OCD, along with Cluster B borderline personality traits.

Psychotherapeutic work was initially focused on conceptualisation based on standard functional analysis, ABC.

Maria's presenting problem was to react with a coping strategy based on A-C, and struggling to identify C (i.e. her emotional states).

Maria's understanding of her own personal perspective and identification of her own self-evaluation and its meaning (i.e. danger, loss, and injustice) supported her own understanding of her own emotional states, resulting in better coping strategies in interpersonal relationships.

References

Alford, B.A., & Beck, A.T. (1997). Therapeutic interpersonal support in cognitive therapy. *Journal of Psychotherapy Integration, 7*(2), 105–117.

Bandura, A. (1977). Self-efficacy: Toward a unifying theory of behavioural change. *Psychological Review, 84*(2), 191–215.

Bandura, A. (1997). *Self-efficacy: The exercise of control.* New York: W.H. Freeman.

Beck, A.T. (1975). *Cognitive therapy and the emotional disorders.* Madison, CT: International Universities Press.

Beck, J.S. (2011). *Cognitive behavior therapy: Basics and beyond.* New York, NY: Guilford Press.

Boniwell, I. (2016). *Positive psychology: Theory, research and applications.* Oxford: McGraw-Hill. Oxford.

Burn, D.D. (1980). *Feeling good.* New York, NY: William Morrow and Company.

Dell'Erba, G.L., Carati, M.A., Greco, S., Muya, M., Nuzzo, E., Gasparre, A.,....Amato, R. (2009). Le convinzioni di dannosità dell'ansia (CDA). *PsicoPuglia,* Ordine Psicologi Puglia, 3.

Dell'Erba, G.L., & Nuzzo, E. (2010). *Psicologia Pratica.* Lecce: Pensa Multimedia.

Dobson, K. (2010). *Handbook of cognitive behavior therapy.* New York, NY: Guilford Press.

Dobson, K. (2011). *Cognitive therapy (Theories of psychotherapy)* (Theories of Psychotherapy Series) Paperback. Washington: American Psychological Assoc.

D'Olimpo, F., & Mancini, F. (2014). Role of deontological guilt in obsessive-cpmpulsive disorder-like checking and washing behavior. *Clinical and Psychological Science, 2,* 727–739.

Ellis, A. (1964). *Reason and emotion in psychotherapy.* New York, NY: Lyle Stuart.

Epictetus. (1865). *The works of epictetus: Consisting of his discourses in four books, the enchiridion, and fragments* (E. Carter & T.W. Higginson, Trans.). Boston, MA: Little, Brown and Co.

Farrand, P. (2020). *Low-intensity CBT skills and interventions a practitioner's manual.* London: Sage.

Hayes S.C., & Hofmann S.G. (2018). *Process based CBT.* Oakland, CA: Context Press, Harbinger.

Hayes, S.C., Strosahal, K.D., & Wilson, K.G. (2012). *Acceptance and commitment therapy.* New York, NY: Guilford Press.

Legrenzi, P. (2019). *Storia della psicologia* (6th ed.). Bologna: Il Mulino.

Miceli, M., & Castelfranchi, C. (2014). *Expectancy & emotions*. Oxford: Oxford University press.

Panksepp, J., & Davis, K. (2018). *The emotional foundations of personality: A neurobiological and evolutionary approach*. New York: W. W. Norton & Company.

Robertson, D. (2019). *The philosophy of cognitive-behavioural therapy (CBT)*. London: Taylor and Francis.

Skinner, B.F. (1975). The shaping of phylogenic behaviour. *Journal of the Experimental Analysis of Behaviours, 24*(1), 117–120.

Warburton, D.A. (2007). *Philosophy: The basics*. London: Routledge.

Weissman, A.N., & Beck, A.T. (1978). *Development and validation of the dysfunctional attitude scale: A preliminary investigation*. Annual Meeting of the American Educational Research Association.

Wells, A. (1997). *Cognitive therapy of anxiety disorders: A practice manual and conceptual guide*. Chichester, UK: Wiley.

Young, J., Klosko, J.S., & Weishaar, M.E. (2003). *Schema therapy. A Practitioner's guide*. New York, NY: Guilford Press.

Chapter 3

Integrative Psychotherapy
Themes in Depth

3.1 Core Beliefs and Rules for Living

Beck (1967) introduced the concept of Core Beliefs or schemas, with the purpose of identifying a framework to individuate, encode, evaluate, and appraise information concerning ourselves as individuals. In Cognitive Therapy, schemas may be verbal or non-verbal and may remain inactive, or triggered by significant events, catalysing several cognitive processes, such as selective attention and memory and problem solving.

Fennell (1997) defined schemas in low self-esteem as deep rooted defeatist beliefs about ourselves, which are void of a wider compassionate sense of self. The schema, or core belief, may be overtly articulated "I am unacceptable," "I'm not good enough," or "I am worthless," for instance. Alternatively, schemas may represent a more generalised "felt sense" of inadequacy. It is worth reflecting that Fennell's model (1997) of low self-esteem is an integration of methods from cognitive therapy for depression, anxiety, and more recent work on schemas.

Our lives are not merely a chronology of events, but meaningful experiences that unfold over time. We experience pivotal events throughout our life, which generate core and generic beliefs about ourselves.

Stories belonging to us are a way to chart a direction, which we undertake based on the meaning attributed by pivotal events.

Meaning turns into choice, or into an answer, that we occasionally attribute to certain facts.

Each one of us follows a path that might be captured by contexts that are more meaningful to him than others.

It is virtually impossible to define, as they would be different for each person.

However, some aspects of our personal experience may be utilised to identify the following themes:

- Vulnerability
- Abandonment

DOI: 10.4324/9781003299226-4

- Inferiority
- Abuse
- Self- Blame
- Diversity

These aspects represent contexts and situations where we may become interpersonally sensitive based on our experiences, meanings, and evaluations generated by such critical events.

From this moment forward, which in theory may be protracted over time, a person might spend his or her life with a focus on protecting themselves from that kind of emotional suffering.

Life stories are ripe with events that create purpose and provide rationale for choices and behaviours; they allow us to comprehend why we suffer and why we behave in certain ways, rather than others (Beck, 2011).

If vulnerability is a predominant theme, then we may focus our attention on certain events rather than others, so we may act by protecting ourselves. However, this will lead to confirm these events as meaningful and recurrent.

We therefore become hypersensitive to certain events and meaning associated with them.

When we "keep an eye" on certain events, we have them constantly on our mind (Wells, 1997).

The pursuit of happiness, the experience of enjoyment, whilst avoiding pain, may be considered one of the final goals of human beings. Human beings who intentionally chose to suffer are a myth: there are reasons that explain why people avoid pain by inflicting themselves pain.

When it comes to suffering, we define what pain is and means to us this may be considered as a theme of our psychological suffering.

Strategies aimed at avoiding distress are known as safety behaviours.

If a person has been humiliated, and this is the key theme of his suffering, he may engage in compensatory strategies-safety behaviours. This may result in the person compromising with negative beliefs and with an unsustainable, dysfunctional sense of self.

Safety behaviours or compensatory strategies do not guarantee effectiveness: there is always going to be the need to push ourselves further, to do more to ensure preventing emotional pain.

For instance, I determine that I will never want to experience a certain event, and move in the opposite direction, to protect myself and prevent any challenges, without knowing where I am heading or where I am directed.

Sustained efforts to distance ourselves from difficult experiences may result in coping dysfunctional behaviours. The function of these behaviours is illusory in nature, and we follow these ideas to ensure our own safety. However, this may result in experiencing further problems.

We therefore avoid and/or ruminate, to prevent perceived catastrophic events in our minds; this results in events becoming more catastrophic and negative.

Throughout time, negative beliefs become extreme and disastrous in nature, leading to generalisations.

For instance, if we determine that we should avoid a situation and anything that resembles it, this will result in an exponential increase of feared events or stimuli, given that the belief/rule "to avoid" what is similar to the feared events, starts from them, but continues to spread, as there is not an established end.

Safety behaviours and compensatory strategies result in behaviours and cognitions that we encounter in clinical practice (Hayes & Hofmann, 2018).

Most psychiatric disorders may be conceptualised as ways of protecting, rescuing, or distancing ourselves from negative beliefs. We might relinquish control to such beliefs, this often occurs in personal crises.

Identification of compensatory strategies and safety behaviours are key themes in recovery from most psychiatric disorders and represent crucial work in psychotherapy (Hayes & Hofmann, 2018).

It is of utter importance to comprehend such dynamics, and to subsequently identify it in our behaviours.

Further focus is placed on identifying underpinning negative beliefs.

In this instance, there are different ways to accept negative events, difficult experiences, faults and other people's responsibility, and our own challenges when dealing with adversity. It is important to repair and reconcile ourselves with other people and (not necessarily on an individual basis), both with us and with how we behaved in difficult moments. This is now referred to as "self-compassion" (Gilbert, 2014).

Lack of ability to reflect and to understand ourselves from a wider perspective, identifying our own behaviours, and the meaning that they acquire, results in struggles in finding our peace.

3.2 The Zeigarnik Effect

The Zeigarnick effect (Dell'Erba & Nuzzo, 2010; Dell'Erba, Carati, Greco, & Muya, 2009; Legrenzi, 2019) is a cognitive process that refers to the tendency to remember and better recall unfinished tasks rather than completed ones.

It is challenging to find inner self-compassion and peacefulness without learning to look within us, our beliefs, and their meaning. Self-reflection and awareness of our own actions directs focus on our values and goals, whereas unresolved difficulties trigger ruminative processes.

Life Themes and safety behaviours have a core process in common: the meaning attributed to significant events. When meaning is attributed in a satisfactory fashion (i.e. we accept what happened and our imperfection as human beings), this might lead to closure and validation of our experience. However, in some instances, validation may be based on feeble and fragile foundations, leaving us with ongoing ruminative efforts to solve and look for an explanation, a life theme, that stems from such events, situations, and our own evaluation.

Unresolved issues may emerge in repetitive ruminative processes, in thought blocking, distractions, and they impose themselves as something that should be closed and archived (Legrenzi, 2019). The obvious solution is to finish our business, but this has to occur in the here and now, through acceptance and a balanced perspective, a wiser version of the unresolved unfinished business.

We often find it essential to experience a pre-existing perspective based on acceptance, by a focus that leads to broadening our perspectives. A perspective that helps to resolve long standing problems and safety behaviours is a common ground within many psychotherapeutic approaches. Contemporary psychoanalysis is based on such stances. Furthermore Cognitive psychotherapies and all the cognitive dynamic approaches are linked to these concepts (Dobson, 2010; Gabbard, 2015). These similarities are hardly acknowledged, as authoritative clinicians tend to brand their own therapeutic and research approaches.

3.3 Model-Based Functional Analyses

Our experiences might be underpinned by certain stimuli, which are the focus of our attention; these generate beliefs, evaluations, feelings, and behaviours linked to such experiences. We previously defined these as Functional Analysis or ABC. The concepts and applications of Functional Analysis (Dobson, 2010) have evolved to conceptualise complex beliefs systems. These can be defined as model-based functional analyses (Hayes & Hofmann, 2018).

For instance, an intrusive obsessional thought is automatic in nature. This creates an Internal Antecedent. This is followed by an Interpretation, a Behaviour, which in turns leads to Consequences, Emotions, in this particular instance. Emotions are directly linked to content generated by B (in this instance, our interpretation). Safety Behaviours follow and correspond to everything that we do as individuals, including reactions to such interpretations, strongly led by emotions.

In this portion of Functional Analysis, we experience different strategies that serve the function to protect us, such as seeking reassurance, acting impulsively on the threat-based interpretation formulated. This might lead to short-term and long-term consequences.

Short-term consequences are immediate. Long-term consequences are characterised by the impact, which is generated some time after the experience or after persistently focusing on such events.

Long-term consequences tend to confirm unhelpful beliefs and interpretations of events.

For instance, long-term consequences linked to avoidance and fear, tell us that we are safe, thus confirming our fears and trapping us. Hence a model based functional analysis captures useful details and relevant psychological processes. Clinical disorders may be effectively conceptualised using these models.

Psychiatric disorders may be grouped in main categories. Single categories lead to classification of more than 300 disorders (American Psychiatric Association, 2012).

Nosography shows us details, but not the general sense of human suffering. Focusing on the content of suffering might lead to creating a potential new mental disorder in future DSM or ICD editions (Bentall, 2009). By contrast, macro-categories allow us to identify similarities between mental disorders and capture the main points, which might help us to treat them. Anxiety Disorders are grouped in a category defined as Anxiety Syndrome. Correspondingly, for Depressive Disorders, we defined a Macro-Category named Depressive Syndrome. We may therefore classify disorders in Macro-Categories (Barlow, Sauer-Zavala, Carl, Bullis, & Ellard, 2014) such as

- Neuro cognitive disorders
- Psychotic disorders
- Depressive disorders
- Anxiety disorders
- Personality disorders

A model based on functional analysis allows us to identify mental processes and features of a vast majority of mental disorders, if we consider their general aspects only.

A person who suffers from an anxiety disorder, may identify an intrusive thought in a certain context, and might interpret it as part of threat based event reacting anxiously, thus acting utilising safety behaviours, based on anxiety driven hypotheses. The person's perception driven hypothesis might then reinforce his anxious predictions.

Diagnosis may depend on specific features of fears of worry, i.e. what is feared, what is meaningful to the individual and how he responds to such a threat. In this instance, an intrusive thought will always be linked with an image linked to catastrophic fears, both directly and indirectly. For instance, a dark spot on the floor might be perceived as blood; therefore, a person may experience worry linked to becoming ill with AIDS, resulting in getting in trouble for being irresponsible, and being blamed for being inadequate.

In Depression, we may interpret boredom as loneliness, and unequivocal abandonment, thus reacting with reassurance seeking behaviours, which will reinforce our perceived inadequacy and result in feeling a victim of being unfairly abandoned.

A sufferer from Psychosis might not be able to recognise an intrusive thought as a thought, but as an external agent of intrusion on his own mind, and therefore misinterpret information that is generated by the external world, rather than his own mind (Beck, 2011). People who suffer from Psychosis would therefore experience thought as being perceived negatively by a public and would react with anger or passivity, with behaviours linked to intrusive thoughts or presumed intrusive thoughts. Behaviours described so far might have consequences that could stop focus on the intrusion (Wells, 2009, 2011), confirming dysfunctional assumptions.

Patients or clients who experience Bulimia Nervosa or Addictions show a propensity to relinquish control of intrusive thoughts and anxious reactions, thus giving themselves permission to act on dysfunctional assumptions, usually linked to temporary relief of suffering. This would be linked to long-term consequences and maintenance of model-based functional analysis.

The implementation of model-based functional analysis includes the following features (Dell'Erba & Nuzzo, 2010; Dell'Erba et al., 2009; Dobson, 2010; Hayes & Hofmann, 2018):

- Attention focused stimulus
- Intrusive Thoughts
- Evaluation
- Emotion
- Safety behaviours
- Consequences

Let's consider where CBT interventions may be positioned in this context. A model-based functional analysis allows a different positioning of CBT interventions.

Mindfulness (Wells, 2011), for instance, could be placed within Attention Focused Stimulus. Mindfulness creates a focus on a stimulus, whether internal or external to our body, whilst creating a non-judgemental stance on processes such as biased evaluations or propensity to react, with associated emotional reactions (Hayes & Hofmann, 2018).

Wells' detached mindfulness provides us with a similar example (Wells, 2011). This intervention allows patients to focus on two or three different stimuli at the same time and notice how their mind does not spiral out of control: this is only apparently opposed to mindfulness.

An Intervention positioned within Intrusive thoughts could be focused on recognition. For instance, notice intrusive thoughts as stimuli without evaluating or judging them.

Evaluation includes interventions focused on analysis of hypotheses and subjective appraisals, along with their foundations. Subjective appraisals might be considered, in this context, the root of these beliefs and their negative evaluations, and challenged as such.

Emotional intelligence means to recognise, understand, and manage our own emotions and attune with others' emotions. Emotions are associated with interventions that have the intent to identify, inform and in some instances, modify emotional reaction. Emotional intelligence is characterised by self-awareness, motivation, empathy and social skills, i.e. Goleman's Emotional Intelligence Goleman (1997).

Safety behaviours include avoidance strategies to protect ourselves from dangers. Exposure based interventions, including Exposure and Response Prevention (ERP) are crucial treatments aimed at addressing these behaviours (Dobson, 2010).

Analysis of long and short-term consequences evaluates the impact of behaviours or solutions to difficulties. Analysis of vicious circles and safety behaviours are also included in functional analyses.

Difficult experiences may be conceptualised as functional analysis and capture mental states, frames of mind, psychological difficulties, characterised by unhelpful beliefs and automatic thoughts and behavioural responses.

Model-based functional analyses (Dell'Erba & Nuzzo, 2010; Hayes & Hofmann, 2018) include a detailed understanding of mental processes linked to:

- External Antecedents – general contexts
- Internal Antecedent – intrusive cognitions
- Direct Behaviour – evaluation and schema
- Reflective Behaviour – identification and integration of metacognition
- Emotional Consequences – emotional state
- Behavioural Consequences – safety behaviours
- Short-term and Long-term consequences

3.4 Conflicts and Core Beliefs

As previously explored, our stories are not just chronologies, but rather perspectives. It is our perspective, at a given point of our lives, which attributes a meaning to our experiences and determines the way forward. Core Beliefs represent part of this story that contributes to clarify our goals and provides a more coherent sense of self. There is an ongoing dynamic tension between such beliefs and events. In fact, we focus on unresolved issues so that we can reconcile our Core Beliefs. This leads us to modify events in order not to compromise our story and identity. We try to protect our Core Beliefs at all costs (2011; Young, Klosko & Weishaar, 2003, Beck, 2011; Young, Klosko, & Weishaar, 2003).

Safety behaviours that are developed to mitigate our suffering, provide a sense of direction and offer solutions. However, they will paradoxically maintain our suffering, through a decrease in flexibility and choices within them. The more profound the suffering, the more rigid and stereotyped are safety behaviours. Non acceptance of risk in certain crucial areas of individual lives becomes an indispensable need characterised by rigid rules. Rigid rules become a way of managing distress intolerance and suffering stemming from negative Core Beliefs (Young et al., 2003).

Such ways of managing distress are transient in nature and are placed within a continuum characterised by acute suffering and feeling of control and self-efficacy: human beings aim to remain within this continuum as it reinforces self-efficacy.

Often events disconfirm a sense of self-efficacy and distancing from psychological suffering. These challenges to safety behaviours are normal; they might, however, represent safety behaviours themselves as they perpetuate aversion to suffering. This results in further suffering as we are scared by further threats, therefore experiencing self-blame or anger. Safety behaviours therefore result in creating a stable negative self-efficacy and become a manifestation of conflict, triggering and perpetuating cyclical ups and downs. One of the most significant aspects of conflict is self-deception.

3.5 Self-Deception

Every human being wishes for happiness or to feel good. However, happiness might be pursued in inflexible ways, almost as a purpose without an end, with no actual meaning or content. A person might alter information in their own lives, to believe that "all is fine."

How is it possible to engage in self-deception? We are not truthful towards ourselves, for a very simple reason: to avoid suffering. However, such an apparently rational process comes at a cost. Self-deception is part of a long-standing philosophical debate, which started from Aristotle (Warburton, 2007). Self-deception has two main features:

1 Deceive ourselves using specific strategies
2 Develop a self-deception strategy to deceive ourselves at any given point in the future (Davidson, 1987; Mele, 2001).

Self-deception is considered an unhelpful way to process and face challenging information: such modality may not be fully accessible by human beings, who may not be fully self-aware, although it might be accessible. However, self-deception makes information harder to process in depth. What kind of form does it take? What are the reasons that lead us to deceive ourselves?

Generally, there are four reasons:

- We are deceitful towards all the problematic aspects, or what we think they are problematic aspects. Those aspects may be related to difficulties that might cause problems at work, within our relationships, our habits, our values
- We deceive ourselves because we want to think positively about ourselves; therefore, we focus on trying to think about ourselves as normal. In particular, we wish to be normal without experiencing any desires, difficulties, passions or repulsions, and intrusive thoughts
- We deceive ourselves as we do not wish to feel inadequate, and below certain standards. In particular, we feel inadequate due to lack or loss of certain things that we consider indispensable
- We deceive ourselves, as we are angry or frustrated towards people, we think we love or we are close to. When we happen to be angry, we also feel confused, guilty, or abnormal, to the point we feel we are the focus of a difficult situation. We attempt to focus on conflict to avoid thinking about or to compromise

The truth about ourselves exposes us to risks with regard to how we perceive ourselves or how we want to feel. We all learn self-deception as we grow and, in fact, we may develop creative ways to deceive ourselves. These ways of deceiving ourselves reveal that the ways in which we may think about ourselves and predisposes us to self-deception are radical and extreme. Any disturbance will create a threat in this context. The purpose of self-deception is to deal with emotional pain and suffering; by contrasting self-awareness, which is crucial to reflect on ourselves, to think, to amend our mistakes, so we can choose a different path in life (Dell'Erba & Nuzzo, 2010; Mele, 2001; Warburton, 2007).

There are several and distinct self-deception strategies, but they may also be seen as a whole (Mele, 2001). Several ways in which we may protect ourselves from facing what causes pain and suffering are avoidance and compensatory strategies.

Every strategy is a blend of behaviours, which aim to compensate, to counterattack, to reclaim something of significant value to us. Strategies that divert us from self-awareness are utilised to face emotional pain: they are characterised by short-term benefits but are not effective in the long-term and they are extremely costly, from a psychological perspective. They make us inflexible, conforming, not keen to grow personally to develop and to learn psychologically and to rectify his own mistakes (Young et al., 2003).

Such self-deceiving behaviours make individuals guarded, hostile, emotionally unavailable. Persisting on such behaviours results in an increase in avoidance of negative beliefs, which in turn increases suffering and difficulties in adapting.

Negative beliefs are present in thoughts, images; they cannot be suppressed or avoided, and tend to re-emerge as mechanisms that have to be closed and completed to be deactivated, like the Zeigarnick effect.

Each person should ascertain that he does not experience "internal alarms," to archive or categorise information as "routine" or "all is going well,", otherwise he would have to focus on preventing threat or loss, until he will find a way to "deactivate the alarm.". Individual might continue to try and find a way to protect himself.

Clearly a self-deceptive option is necessary when psychological suffering is intense and represents a core aspect for the person (Arntz & Lobbestael, 2018; Young et al., 2003). Often innocent self-deception characterises our psychological "normality" as in we do not have to be rigorous in all aspects of our inner life. Avoiding delaying with this is not an efficient or effective way of dealing with this, at least in the medium to long-term.

The cost we pay to maintain such a defensive stance is ongoing tension and hypervigilance, like a sentinel waiting for the enemy: it has a physical and physiological cost.

How can we reframe this?

We may find the courage to deal with what seems to be an obstacle, or a frustration, reminding ourselves that we do not have to behave like super-human beings.

What Nietzsche suggested was to free ourselves from deception and to become superhuman, but this does not seem to be feasible or realistic (Robertson, 2019). Rather we can improve according to what is within our power and remain flexible and oriented towards what is important to us, without being heroes or blaming ourselves, with humility.

Self-deception in its purest form is not usually experienced by individuals who do not suffer from mental health disorders (Mele, 2001). There are three important factors to consider.

1 Self-deception is a normal psychological process (i.e. Taylor, 1989) and her work on Positive Illusions); it can become radicalised in certain circumstances, due to a person excessively investing in shielding and protecting himself and his true intentions, which may be challenged or threatened by any trigger.
2 Understanding the key features of excessive defensiveness and self-deception; arguably these may be linked to acceptance and/or facing reasons behind suffering.

3 Prolonged avoidance, distraction, and resistance to think about uncomfortable or challenging issues are incredibly difficult, almost impossible, to sustain. This is a classic cognitive therapy standpoint, i.e. Wegner, Schneider, Carter, and White (1987) and his experiments on thought suppression (i.e. white bear; Wegner & Schneider, 2003).

3.6 Suffering and Internal Conflictual Dynamic

Burdensome experiences may be conceptualised as ABCs. Recurrent meanings related to intrusive thoughts are linked to painful life themes, from which individuals wish to detach themselves, thus creating dichotomous perspectives, and conflict between coping and consequences between different mental states. Where do negative beliefs originate from? We are entering the realm of psychological vulnerability and emotional suffering.

Causes of emotional suffering are multifaceted. However, these are narrowed down when we focus on psychological suffering. This starts by defining the meaning of psychological suffering. Suffering is the perception of pain, for example, physical pain. This is purely descriptive, i.e. pain may be described as an internal body signal, a sensor that transmits it and a receptor that receives it. Different is the problem of suffering, or rather to experience pain.

For instance, if we experience physical pain as suffering, we may or may not be fully self-aware of the extent to which we gauge whether we can tolerate or not tolerate pain. In the latter instance, we might experience both pain and avoidance of pain, as a coping mechanism.

When referring to psychological suffering instead, we do not allude to physical pain, but to negative emotions. What is causing suffering is linked to the belief that we will lose something crucially important, something we are trying to acquire or pursue through an action plan.

We suffer as we consider this action plan under threat, both in the present and in the future, and we evaluate action plan consequences as potential threats also.

If such an action plan is evaluated as less important, then our suffering will decrease. If we consider the action plan as irreplaceable, and consequences of its loss as intolerable and unstainable, then our suffering will increase. Thus, psychological suffering is linked to emotions experienced by us as human beings. We suffer due to the belief of losing or considering what we value the most, what is good, and the benefits associated with what we consider good.

Our personal values and Core Beliefs, and how we evaluate and judge ourselves, represent a key aspect of our sense of self as human beings. It is a core cultural and evolutionary aspect (Arntz & Lobbestael, 2018; Hayes, Strosahal, & Wilson, 2012).

Some set beliefs may be depicted as follows: if you produce something, then you are a worthy being; if you work, then you are a worthy being; if you work well then you are worthy; if you are good at school, then you are worthy; if you are good at sports then you are worthy; we create rules that influence our worth as human beings. We are only worthy if such rules are adhered to and requirements related to the rules are met.

We then focus on rules that make it possible for us to be worthy. These may work well for us, with luck and for a certain period of time. However, a sudden event may occur and threaten our sense of self or Core Beliefs. This leads us to avoid, or to engage in compensatory behaviours based on self- deception.

It is essential to learn to challenge the belief that we are worthy only based on certain canons and the contexts where we learn them, as canons or rules create vulnerability and predisposition to psychological suffering. A further cause of psychological suffering might be our difficulties in learning self-control and regulation (Hayes et al., 2012). We can build awareness and control on certain events, but we are also aware that we have no power over other events.

Excluding discerning what we can, from what we cannot control, can influence goals which we set and aspire to, or conversely, we may choose not to pursue. Reversing this concept means to pursue what is out with our control. This aspect represents the quintessence of our psychological suffering. An important point to consider is that in general we all rely and depend on chance and other people. It is at this precise point that we reflect on what we can do, what is in our power to pursue or achieve our goal.

When this reflection morphs into a demand, it becomes "We must achieve our goal." However, we will emotionally suffer if this will be out of our control (unrealistic aim or intent).

In some instances, it might become very important for our identity and sense of Self-Worth to have certain goals, which will have consequences (generally linked to emotional suffering), for instance, to avoid thinking about grief. When a loved one passes away, a person may think that the deceased is still present in his life or suppress the thought of grief altogether. This results in development of further psychological problems, or unrealistic expectations. These kinds of goals may be incongruous with each other, thus causing confusion and despondency. Furthermore, strategies aimed at a rapid resolution and at not suffering, might seem actual solutions, when they in fact perpetuate s problems and suffering.

Letting go of a goal is not easy: at the core of this decision, there has to be a rational conceptualisation based on psychological information. How do I know that I may not control my thoughts? How do I know that grief and its processes require time? Furthermore, how may I understand that information is constantly resurfacing on my minding? Understanding psychological processes, if not psychotherapy, is our best solution at these times.

Personal values and control determine the necessity to justify our own suffering, conceptualising it as our Negative Core Beliefs (Alford & Beck, 1997). Where does individual psychological suffering originate from?

One of psychotherapy's intent is to re-evaluate some critical events, where subjective evaluation is directed to a stereotypical lack of success (failure) of vulnerability factors.

As discussed by Barlow (2010) and Dell'Erba and Nuzzo (2010), the dimensions of Agency and Communion summarise various factors linked to psychological vulnerability, as already identified in Beck's Cognitive Theory of Depression (Alford & Beck, 1997).

How can we outline the variables that may support a conceptualisation of suffering from a trans-theoretical perspective? Generally, we may reflect that suffering is determined by struggles:

- To accept frustration
- To accept what is within our control and what is not
- To rely on Core Beliefs regardless as to whether we experience negative or positive experiences

In more detail, we can identify four general areas that are associated with suffering:

- The need to be well and experience positive emotions
- The need for approval and to be evaluated positively
- The need to avoid feared negative events
- The need to avoid negative evaluations towards ourselves (Hayes et al., 2012).

We can refer to such areas as follows:

1 I want to feel X (or I do not want to feel Y)
2 I want S to think X (or he does not think Y)
3 I want to have X (or not to have Y) and I cannot have it
4 I do not want to think about X (or to think about Y), I cannot do so.

These goals appear impossible to achieve and may be in turn translated into the following strategies aimed at inflexible control:

- Control our emotions and our emotional state
- Control other people's opinions
- Control future events and eventual frustration and pain
- Control our own thoughts.

These areas may affect psychological aspects of change.

Let's focus on the Mind and of ABC: how may we envisage a B overflowing information?

ABC is heuristic, practical, and created to be utilised to work on cognitions (Dobson, 2010).

The first necessary step is indeed, meaning. When we experience a problem or frustration as a Consequence, it is important to understand what it is like for this individual to experience that problem.

A second step is to identify an ulterior meaning, which is, however, related to the fact we are experiencing the problem in the first instance: we will define this as "secondary problem."

Often the "secondary problem" focus is to experience a given Consequence or rather a certain emotion (anxiety, shame, guilt, sadness, envy). Or to have thought x or y, or have behaved in a certain way (i.e. inhibited, irritated, rude, etc.).

A third step is the idea that our patients have a problem and that affects their mental state. Here we identify Negative Beliefs, or we can identify Rules for Living (Young et al., 2003).

A fourth step is characterised by Interpersonal Schemas or reasons why we utilise certain coping strategies. At this level, we access subjective and inflexible rules that have their core in the Negative Beliefs (Arntz & Lobbestael, 2018; Young et al., 2003).

A fifth step is concerned with our story, key memories and events, which often confirm choices and schemas, and initial rules inferred by meaning attributed to critical events. These events represent a reappraisal of our mind now, of the meaning given by our "yesterday's mind" (Dell'Erba & Nuzzo, 2010).

To conclude, we may discover different layers within ourselves, which may lead to developing many interventions. Some are more immediate and some more sophisticated and meaningful at a personal level.

3.7 Self-Serving Bias, Consciousness, and Self-Consciousness

Self-Serving Bias is one of the most studied psychological processes (Legrenzi, 2019; Pedrini, 2019). Self-Serving Bias is a self-protection mechanism that serves the function to safeguard ourselves from threats posed to our Self-Worth or Conditional Beliefs (Dell'Erba & Nuzzo, 2010; Pedrini, 2019).

How do we link protection and safeguarding of our own self-esteem to our Core Beliefs? Some people are hypersensitive towards failures and therefore evaluate small and temporary faults, as indicators of lack of worth or lack of Self-Worth. Many others do not experience this problem.

Normally most of us have developed resilience towards small failures or faults. Each individual has an inner "program," albeit not a conscious level, that tends to protect his self-esteem. Such "program" manipulates information related to faults and failures or related to merit and qualities (Miceli & Castelfranchi, 2014).

Self-Serving Bias re-evaluates threats and attempts to re-adjust our sense of worth in a more benevolent manner, minimising the importance of faults, and increasing our qualities and merit, thus producing protective explanations for what happened. Thus, Self-Serving Bias occurs when we consider ourselves in danger to experience ourselves as total failures, or completely unlovable and therefore seeing our Self Worth damaged.

A different way, as previously discussed, consists in considering a human being not appraisable as a Human Being, thus decreasing the meaning of such evaluation.

It is crucial to be self-aware in this context. We may be conscious of this, and place such consciousness in a continuum, as in self-focused attention or in a threatening situation.

Being conscious means that we perceive something. Being self-aware means something more complex.

We are not always aware and in contact with stimuli and reality around us. Some behaviours are merely habits, and all information is gathered automatically, not immediately and not even in a self-aware fashion.

Whilst it is important that we complete tasks as part of routines and as a habit, given that it is thanks to this process that we increase our range of actions, it would not be possible to act in a robotic way and have everything under control.

Semi-conscious routines are an achievement of our species. Also, to function on autopilot might make things worse. For instance, reacting to intrusive thoughts and negative emotions using our autopilot modality is likely to make us feel worse and position ourselves far from our valued sense of direction.

It is essential to notice our autopilot mode, as it relies on the idea that we have about how our mind operates, or a model of the mind, for those who are not experts in this field. Our ability to recognise such therapeutic modality means to identify parameters and warning signs that we can utilise to our advantage. It is useful to occasionally disengage from the automatic pilot, so we may choose what we would like to do in a given situation. Our mind, part of our attention, explores past and future scenarios, as in time travel. These scenarios are appraised and evaluated as a foundation to reason and extrapolate solutions; such solutions or rules may also be particularly inflexible and unchallengeable. Furthermore, they are activated by threats posed to our aims and goals.

Yielding control of our actions or choices to such rules leads to negative, stressful outcomes and psychological impoverishment, and it positions ourselves farther away from our valued sense of direction. It is crucial that we develop the skill to regulate self-awareness.

Developing self-awareness may acquire several meanings and different aims and intents, either practical or clinical.

Mindfulness techniques (Baer, 2018; Hayes et al., 2012) aim to develop skills that can lead us away from autopilot, either by practising regular interventions or therapeutic tasks linked to connect ourselves to the present moment. Practising mindful self-awareness increases our ability to detach ourselves from repetitive unhelpful narratives that surround our minds, our prejudices, judgements and images that our minds produce on past and present scenarios. Detaching ourselves from inflexible rules, allows us to connect with the present, and to strengthen our ability to choose and act.

We can consider two different perspectives – a Thinking Self or an Observing Self. These are a well-known concept in philosophy and psychology (Hayes & Hofmann, 2018).

From an Observing Self-perspective, the experience is virtually non-stop, with a plurality of information, and vast access to our experiences. From this perspective, it is reasonably clear that we cannot be defined by specific judgments, or statements, or specific criteria. This means that we exist as Observing beings (i.e. we experience perception), "a part of me is cognizant and conscious of the other part of me." Thus judgements, emotions, a memory, a comment, represent stimuli that we may notice, perceive and observe; they constitute part of our overall experience, along with all of the other stimuli (Baer, 2018).

From an observer's perspective, we may choose how to act and how to respond to our own mind's hypotheses, memories, fantasies, and the wanderings of our imagination.

Choosing how to respond to such experiences is very different from attempting to control them, or to act as if these features were rules or commands.

Observing Self-Perspective is a modality of the mind that makes effective choices possible, especially with regard to what the individual deems important long term. This stance is much more reliable and contained than a stance focused on alarm.

Choosing what is important or meaningful to us is very different from trying to control negative emotions, intrusive thoughts, and associated physical symptoms. This might represent a temporary relief, albeit a long-term trap. This kind of approach to consciousness is well received and effective in the treatment of many mental disorders (Hayes & Hofmann, 2018).

To become aware that a part of ourselves creates or elaborates information is pivotal. We may evaluate those mental processes for objective information, rather than being spontaneous thoughts, fantasies, or prejudices.

Many individuals believe that negative thoughts or unpleasant emotions, or simply stress, are psychological states to eliminate quickly; otherwise, they might adversely impact on their well-being and their intent to live a good life. However, although involuntary negative thoughts and unpleasant emotions are manifestations of a challenge, they do not represent the real threat, only an associated warning sight, like the fuel light. Wanting to rid ourselves of negative thoughts and emotions paradoxically results in experiencing more intrusive thoughts and unpleasant emotions. Furthermore, increasing our efforts to control these thoughts may create a further psychological problem, along with frustration of not being able to control a part of ourselves. This can significantly scare and dishearten us.

At the core of this perspective, there is a naïve theory of the mind, typical of children, less so in adults, and definitely present in many of our patients and clients. This is a feature of metacognitive nature, which is originated by rules and information that do not factor in how an alarmed and scared mind operates.

In particular, human beings find it hard to consider how their mind functions when they experience intense emotions (Alford & Beck, 1997). In fact, these specific aspects morph into specific problems with related dysfunctional coping behaviours. Individuals may often mistake spontaneous thoughts, with the evaluation or judgement that they attribute to any events, or situations.

We might also evaluate our own spontaneous imagination; a negative evaluation results in attempts to eradicate such thoughts, as if they were entirely under our control. This might result in an intensification of spontaneous thoughts, which will become more intrusive and intense, with additional negative evaluation stemming from perceived failure – for not being able to control and regulate our emotions and cognitions – associated with frustration.

The more elements we add, the more the predisposition to create complex and layered psychological problems increases. A common denominator in these kinds of psychological problems is the excess of control, of something that cannot be controlled. The alternative to this safety behaviour is willingness to experience frustration, and to allow our mind, or part of ourselves, to function normally.

Our willingness to allow our mind to function in such a way is associated both to the degree of knowledge that we have of our minds – despite not being psychologists, and to the kind of objectives and expectations that we have about ourselves, and our functioning.

In other words, the problem is not the frustration, but the meaning we attribute to it, and what we want or better, what we expect (i.e. not just our goals, but the way we pursue our goals).

Psychological suffering is characterised by individuals' goals and specifically by what he requires to be "OK," and by the ability, or lack thereof, to reflect on them, and adopt a flexible, less rigid, more adaptable stance.

What creates inflexibility results in individuals becoming fixed on unhelpful choices and allows them to morph into Needs and Musts. Individuals should not define their sense of Self-Worth based on the achievement of rigid life goals (Alford & Beck, 1997).

Values and Self-Worth are highly meaningful abstractions, but they are not objects or facts. Nothing that can happen to individuals can directly compromise their Self-Worth or the pursuit of their Values.

This can be summarised in the following manner.

It is important to live according to X; therefore, as a human being "I am interested in doing my best in working towards X." Whilst X is a value, X can be objectives that are linked to meaningful values, their sensible direction, the path which individuals flexibly undertake. It is meaningful to encourage a person to manage a different part of his or her mind and its functioning. A work focused on the discovery of the self.

The willingness to allow part of our mind and body to engage in normal processes, is crucial to identify, or at least, perceive such processes with distance and curiosity (Hayes et al., 2013). This is defined as metacognitive identification (Wells, 2008). This means observing how we think from an "external observer" perspective, i.e. in a distanced way, as Beck theorised in the first instance (Hayes, 2019).

Our ability to be aware of part of our mental processes may develop, nurture, and rehabilitate when, after long periods of psychological suffering, we experience a decrease in such ability. It is worth reflecting that engaging in metacognitive processes is challenging for individuals who suffer from mental health disorders (Cupitt, 2019; Lysaker & Klion, 2018).

Willingness to experience intrusive and spontaneous thoughts (positive, neutral, or negative), negative or positive emotions, physical symptoms associated with physical conditions, is a choice that can be routinely practised, such as consistent, rather than inconsistent training (Hayes et al., 2012). The key factor in the development of this ability is to notice mental processes without attempting to control them, and this might facilitate our own conscious focus.

In Mindfulness training, we frequently notice consciousness linked to planning, followed by an evaluating consciousness only, which is followed by consciousness, which does not plan or evaluate (Baer, 2018).

When Mindfulness training is delivered inconsistently, this process is not fully achieved, as individuals might still be engaged in certain cognitive processes, instead of considering them nonjudgmentally.

When we lack distance towards these mental processes, we may be trapped into intrusive thoughts, feelings, or meaning attributed to them, memories, or hypotheses (Hayes et al., 2012).

It may be useful to remember that all of these considerations affect our overall psychological functioning, where the core aspect is represented by the meaning that we attribute to our feelings, emotions, memories, imagination.

In advanced Mindfulness practice, we might be able to notice the vehicle that transports information, but without any information, for instance, we can recall an occurrence without attributing any meaning to it.

We continue to learn that we are observing mental processes, and not facts or events that are occurring in the here and now, towards which we might react.

Practising presence in the here and now and noticed in a non-judgemental way is part of a new CBT approach, somehow inspired directly or indirectly by mindfulness, but at their core they possess the important characteristics of psychology of consciousness (Hayes & Hofmann, 2018).

3.8 Focus on Well-Being

It is plausible to consider metacognition and psychological self-regulation's contribution to our everyday living problems, given that it is utilised for mental health disorders. This is an aspect concerned with opportunities to prevent and minimise likelihood of mental health disorders, for the individual benefit and his good psychological functioning.

How might we summarise the development of a serious psychological disorder? In the first instance, it is important to reflect that to live also means to suffer, although not entirely suffering (Hayes et al., 2012). Suffering is part of living and is also an integral part of problem solving. In such instances, we can define Frustration emotions linked to unachieved goals.

The specific meaning of the importance of such intentions might label specific emotions such as worry, guilt, shame, and sadness. Temporary frustration is part of our lives, as it is to pursue what we deem important. If "I do not feel, I do nothing. I do not react to threats, dangers, to what can kill me." Thus, frustration is a normal emotion to what is not matching our expectations.

Problems cause stress, and therefore, we focus on trying to solve them; otherwise, they take for granted that they become part of our routine. This process might result in employing our mental energy or resources to solve them (for instance, do two or more things at the same time). Problems may also be related to changes. Changing something implies effort on different levels; therefore, changes are usually loaded with stress, which, however, has a beginning and an end.

We all find a way to adapt to a new equilibrium and new macro- and micro-routines. Sometimes we deal with changes that require a temporary detour from our goals and direction and this can be stressful and frustrating. We place our best efforts in establishing a valued sense of direction and to maintain such direction. Hence, why "detours" are stressful.

When focusing on our valued sense of direction we try to ensure that we maintain our psychological well-being. Good psychological maintenance means to abide to two main principles:

- Pursue our values within what is in our power, and not in what is not possible
- Nothing holds to our Sense or Worth

We might face challenges and difficult moments throughout our lives, these can test us, and result in doubting our Self-Worth and ability to self-regulate. We also could define a critical incident as something intolerable and catastrophic, paired with lack of encouragement, i.e. lack of Agency and/or Communion.

If we are unable to reframe those critical incidents and adapt, we might feel in danger and will therefore respond with avoidance strategies, which with time might also affect remaining aspects of personal life.

Seligman's Causal Attribution Theory (Seligman, 1991) claims that we will cease to attempt to change our circumstances if we deem them to be out of our control. How do we attribute causality and control in mediating our mental states? This model includes three causal explanatory dimensions of attribution:

- Stable/unstable causes
- Internal/external causal statements
- Global-specific causal explanations

If an individual frames an event as specific, external, and temporary, the event will be reframed and solved with problem solving and adapting; whereby global, internal, and permanent causa's individual attributions, might lead to a different problem. When an individual evaluates a critical incident as something that challenges what is important to him, including what he believes about himself, he will tend to believe that a negative outcome will be likely and will likely attempt to avoid it.

Logically there is a difference between avoiding a specific negative event versus something that is perceived as global, and therefore a vague threat. In the first instance, a person becomes more inflexible, as he has to protect himself from what is negative. We defined this as a negative core belief (negative theme).

Human beings tend to protect themselves from frustration originated from negative experiences by employing onerous and massive strategies or might otherwise yield to negative schema, thus decreasing functioning in areas of their lives.

We may recognise features of specific mental disorders, such as anxiety or depressive disorders, or the first symptoms of personality disorders, eating disorders or substance misuse, in context of decreased functioning.

Mental disorders are usually intertwined with self-criticism, discouragement, and sometimes, resentment and hostility. All of these factors contribute to imprisoning people in problematic situations. Psychological problems might then become psychological traps (Dell'Erba & Nuzzo, 2010; Johnson-Laird, Mancini, & Gangemi, 2006).

3.9 Psychological Traps

What are good psychological therapy ingredients that may support individuals to free themselves from psychological traps? firstly, the therapeutic relationship and the opportunity to establish mutual collaboration with our patient and clients (Sturmey & Hersen, 2012).

In fact, an integrative aspect concerning the therapeutic relationship is the space where patients' problems are evidenced in patterns. Working on such patterns is innovative and effective (Safran & Muran, 2000; Carcione, Niccolò, & Semerari, 2016). A common denominator is to consider the therapeutic relationships as an opportunity to work on the unhelpful Patterns in session.

A second factor is exquisitely technical and concerns that ability to promote individuals' ability to understand how our mind functions, what is happening and support to identify what really is important to him, excluding of course, dysfunctional coping (Hayes et al., 2012).

A third factor is fostering the development of psychological abilities and accepting our thoughts and constructively challenging them in keeping with our personal and meaningful choices (Dahl, Plumb, Stewart, & Lundgren, 2009).

A fourth factor is to understand the model of the problem (Barlow, Allen, & Choate, 2004). This particular point can be different, according to the psychotherapeutic modality employed. It is pivotal to discern between the following:

- What is linked to our mind and its content and what he believes and feels regarding the problems that he is facing – Schema and Database
- Awareness of what is happening and what can be perceived – Online Input
- What is really important to him – Life Goals

Within all these facets lie the aspects of applied CBT, such as behavioural experiments, exposure, cognitive restructuring techniques in its various forms.

A further important factor is the identification and exploration of what is important for individuals, their realistic objectives in relation to their own life values.

Self-Worth should be reframed as essential for a human being and freed from attributed meanings and rigid goals.

Resilience and its core aspects, i.e. making realistic plans and carrying them out, manage our feelings, and impulses in a healthy manner and confidence in our strengths and abilities.

At this point, we would like to reflect on experiential avoidance, a core construct of Third Wave therapies, particularly explored by the Acceptance Commitment Therapy- ACT (Hayes et al., 2012).

Experiential avoidance is a form of resistance to experience negative emotions, sensations, cognitions, or memories. It is an attempt to avoid negative and undesired mental states.

Furthermore, experiential avoidance is a predisposing factor in the vast majority of mental disorders. This stance is not only considered unpleasant, abnormal, and intolerable, but also an external object or an event that is possible to control. Unfortunately, our internal experiences such as fantasies, intrusive thoughts, emotions, or memories, along with physical symptoms, are not subjected to our control and are not within our power (Hayes et al., 2012).

Our attempts to resist these experiences as they are manifested make our way of feeling and think as an adverse stimulus, and the associated mental state as abnormal; this is what creates psychological traps.

Reversing experiential avoidance results in creating acceptance, as a frame of mind to make ourselves available to experience these events as normal and part of our beings (Dahl et al., 2009).

In fact, we might also consider that within ourselves there is a stance designed to avoid internal experiences, where in fact our dysfunctional part makes it challenging to achieve our valued sense of direction.

Factors that regulate the relationship between a person and the external world are not unlimited. Our psychological life, with its richness and variety, could be explained by a defined series or general processes. There are three main groups of processes that regulate our psychological life (Dell'Erba & Nuzzo, 2010; Hayes & Hofmann, 2018).

- Mental processes related to coding, memory, cognitive schemas, knowledge, and all variables that may be included in a database
- Conscience, which we experience in relation to internal and external stimuli, and how we may remain aware observers, whilst not losing our conscience as thinking individuals
- Processes and functions that regulate behaviours and motivation, particularly constructive motivation, needs, and meaningful aims.

Those macro processes act synergically and originate behaviours and/or complex life plans.

In this context, such mental processes and variables of psychological life may represent both therapeutic actions and traps in the context of psychological suffering.

Such overall vision brings a view which is undeniably pragmatic and heuristic advantage, perhaps to the detriment of richness of details.

3.10 Improving Meta-Cognitive Difficulties

There are several ways to identify and treat meta-cognitive difficulties of our patients and clients. These can be categorised as follows (Dell'Erba & Nuzzo, 2010; Hayes et al., 2012):

- Metacognitive awareness
- Metacognitive knowledge
- Metacognitive strategies

We may experience difficulties in understanding our own mind and psychological processes, as we may be too naïve, or we struggle to identify emotions or mental states, to acknowledge and recognise them in people, or even to act in a manner congruent with our experienced difficulties.

What are the factors that may decrease individuals' abilities to comprehend his own or other individuals' mind? There may be several.

Firstly, brain deficits are the neurobiological basis of our consciousness, and the external world lies (Lysaker & Klion, 2018). Such deficits may be very specific. Furthermore, emergency or emotionally charged situations may decrease our metacognitive ability.

This seems to be related to challenges posed in processing information overload, whereby our knowledge system can only process information related to survival.

Another factor is decreased interpersonal skills, due to a developmental history characterised by severe abuse and neglect from caregivers, where interpersonal and psychological repair also lacked (Lysaker & Klion, 2018).

Lastly, a dysfunctional understanding of our interpersonal world and functioning, of our minds, and interpersonal relationships; these factors may be correlated to keeping individuals isolated from a wider sociocultural environment (Beck et al., 2008).

We may define metacognitive context as understanding our own and others' mind, to be able to live a fulfilling life.

Although there are different metacognitive conceptualisations, there is enough consensus in differentiating 3–4 general factors, with their own distinct features (Tarricone, 2011).

- Understand our own mind – Self-reflexivity
- Understand others' mind – Theory of Mind
- Face relational/interpersonal problems – Mastery

Several authors are specifically researching metacognitive features and constructs in psychotherapy or psychopathology, which may be leading to finding different coding and languages (Carcione et al., 2016).

A classic metacognitive difficulty would be the uncertainty in discerning the difference between external mental events. A classic symptom of psychosis, for instance, is much more endemic at a micro level than what is normally envisaged. A variant of this aspect is the differentiation between Events and Thoughts, or between Perceived External World and our Inner Internal World (within our mind).

Mental state difficulties that we may experience towards our or other people's minds may be categorised as follows (Carcione et al., 2016):

- Lack of differentiation between perception of emotions, and the evaluation that determines the same. This is the prerequisite for CBT's ABC
- Identification of specific emotion vs a sense of uneasiness, unwellness, or stress. This kind of confusion and lack of understanding is recognisable in the alexithymia patient (such terminology is now outdated – see DSM 5)
- Lack of differentiation between others and our own perspective. This is a crucial factor in several psychopathological models. The difference between understanding ourselves and others is also related to our ability to discern between the perspectives that we adopt, as Piaget indicated in his work. According to Piaget, children's ability to see colours on the side of the pyramid, beside what they see in front of them is a good model to refer to someone else's mind (Smith, Bem, & Nolen-Hoeksema, 2004)

David Premack (Premack & Premack, 1983) defined this as Theory of Mind – he initially referred to chimpanzees. However, the term was later used extensively (Smith et al., 2004). Features of Theory of Mind include

- Discernment of the differences between our own and other people's opinions is the foundation not to argue with others, or to understand how other people feel. All of these aspects require development of strategies that are utilised based on such perspectives. It should be noted that if underlying abilities are dysfunctional, so will be strategies
- The contrast between Past and Present. A memory may evoke a painful scenario, and unresolved issues that cause suffering. However, it is important to consider that this is in the past, not in the present. Not in

the present means that the negative scenario is unfolded within our own minds and does not co-exist with us; this is not as clichéd as we may think

- Dissimilitude between rigid and flexible evaluations. Such dissimilitude is not operated between evaluations as such, but is a mental process which should, however, be identified with individuals. It should therefore be identified as metacognitive knowledge, so this can make it possible to appraise such evaluation as extreme. The underlying mechanism here is the catastrophic misinterpretation, as a core psychopathological feature. The presence of such dichotomous thinking style highlights the presence of alarming threatening consequences
- Variance between our self-evaluations that can be global or specific, according to Seigman's Attributional Theory (Seligman, 1990). This variance is mostly related to our Self Worth
- Differentiation between ourselves and others, from a cursory perspective, behavioural and contextual, rather than based on attributions based on conceptualising behaviours as mental states. We define this as Mentalisation (Allen, Fonagy, & Bateman, 2008). One of the key aspects of Mentalisation is the parental ability of a mother to interact with her own child as a being with a mind, thus interacting meaningfully and intentionally, rather than superficially. A variant of Mentalisation is the mental ability to discern between the Self and the Mind; between myself talking and the mind processes, for instance
- Dissimilitude between Dissociation and Self-Consciousness. In Dissociation, we are hyper involved with current stimulus, without any fluctuation of the consciousness of focus on the me as an observer, and the issues that recall certain scenarios. In Self-Consciousness, our attention focus is shifted to me as an observer, thus blurring what we perceive and the context. This is a particular relevant point, as it is challenging for patients who suffer from dissociative post-traumatic events. At its core is, however, normal for mental states to shift focus from observing self and stimuli that are at the basis of depersonalisation and derealisation, which result in loss of metacognitive ability of learning how our mind works and mistake such focus for alarming symptoms
- To conclude, we may differentiate between referring to ourselves within our own ABC, in relation to reference to ourselves bearing in mind ongoing patterns, and our personal story. Such perspective embodies a particularly complex and integrative perspective within us

The vast majority of patients and clients who undergo psychotherapy struggle to engage in these ABCs, and it is this aspect that probably leads to the development of psychological traps and psychological disorders (Hayes & Hofmann, 2018).

3.11 Levels of Consciousness

The classic definition of conscious and unconscious is somewhat peculiar. Contemporary models utilise unconscious factors as mechanisms and trends characterised by meanings that act as a means to a purpose (Legrenzi, 2019).

The majority of psychotherapeutic therapeutic models adopt a functional macro- model (Barlow et al., 2004; Hayes & Hofmann, 2018).

It would be important to re-define the difference between conscious and unconscious, to what aspects of mental processes they refer to. Some aspects of the mind are not captured from a subjective perspective. Some others are automatic, but may they become the focus of our attention, and are therefore conscious.

For instance, if I see a snake, I already know that it means danger, and I get into fight or flight response. I am conscious of the snake, and conscious of my reaction and I might be conscious that it is fear. I am not conscious of the way in which I manifest my fear, but I can become so, whilst I am experiencing this.

A propensity to act may become conscious when it is being actioned, before then it is just a possibility. As in a computer program, which establishes conditions, so that x can occur; otherwise, y occurs instead.

Habits operate in a similar manner and play a crucial role in optimising individual resources, so that we may function efficiently and therefore survive.

Several habits are automatic, although they might become the focus of our attention and therefore become conscious. We cannot change our behaviour if it does not become the focus of our attention (Dobson, 2010). However, to modify a habit, a routine, I have to stop certain ways in which I optimise my attention and mental resources.

When I stop a habit, I might become stressed. This is because a habit or a routine results in minimising efforts in information processing, breaking it down in chunks, in a way that other information is considered similar. When I stop this process, I might stop optimising my resources, thus causing stress. This results in worry or despondency.

When I learn to play tennis, my game efficiency will be linked to my specific ways of playing. A tennis coach might inform me that I have to change the way I plan. When I train to correct my techniques as advised, I might experience stress, as I have to modify an optimised habit. Training step by step, I will learn a new way of playing, and will create a new routine for a new habit.

Automatic pilots are behaviours or thoughts in which we engage without thinking about them fully, as if we are driving on a straight motorway, part of our mind is engaged in other processes, other than driving. Sometimes this may be a constructive and efficient process, other times it can become limited and stereotyped.

A way to rectify the danger to minimise the likelihood to become involved in an accident is to focus on a marker so our attention can be focused on what we are actually doing and change our behaviours. Similarly, in order to change a behaviour, I need to understand what indicates the problem and the autopilot should be stopped as our attention is focused on the pilot. If I am reading, but I focus on something that happened in the past, I will be unable to complete my reading. I need to focus on the task and let go of past events, at least temporarily let go of past episodes, which can be resolved or dealt with at a later stage.

3.12 Active Mind vs Proactive Mind

The link between philosophy, stoicism, psychology, and psychotherapy is embodied within the tendency to anticipate events, not just perceive them and evaluate them through a schema or a bias, however functional or dysfunctional they may be.

When we refer to ABC, or a snapshot related to problematic events, what we have in mind is a causal arrow, which can be inflexibly casual or simply temporary. Such arrow follows a stimulus-based flow that experimental psychologists are so fond of, throughout one hundred years of psychology as a scientific discipline. In the same experimental tradition, there is a psychological "fact" that goes in the opposite direction.

A stimulus A is interpreted as B and determines an emotional response C. Individuals implicit and explicit knowledge are proactively oriented towards expectations, hypotheses, beliefs, projected, and applied to future situations. In our mind, we have an ever-active cognitive device that anticipates events; it has significant advantages in evolutionary terms and in everyday life. However, it also has costs, as it might not always accurately conceptualise perceptual knowledge (Miceli & Castelfranchi, 2014).

Perceptive heuristics is characteristic of normal individuals, and inherent to cognitive processes.

Proactivity of mind is crucial when we consider expectations as an integral part of the psychology of suffering (Miceli & Castelfranchi, 2014). A psychological focus on a proactive mind enriches psychological explanatory strength.

What is the nature of some of the most basic mental processes or main aspects of human psychology?

What if Perception represents much less of a copy of what is in the present, rather than a slight hallucination or delusion as to what to expect?

What if Memory were not a photograph archive, but a collection of opportunities?

What if Emotions were not a mere agitation in the present moment, but rather a guide for future expectations?

What if Happiness were not a current state of the art report, but a forecast for the future?

What if Morality were not an evaluation of present action, but future actions of individuals?

What if Psychotherapy were less of an attempt to solve past conflicts, and rather a way to change a way in which an individual can face the present and future?

What if our Mind were not a source and depository of knowledge, but an engine that has the power to predict?

What would happen to our view of psychology, had we not been driven by the past and attracted to the future? And for each one of us, what kind of future?

These are some ideas that aid understanding of psychology as an ever-growing discipline.

The propensity to utilise or to employ a proactive perspective, is a clear and pragmatic outline.

Let us focus on how we may explore proactive stances more in depth.

Epictetus differentiated between what is within our control and what is not (Robertson, 2019). The corollary that follows is that we can focus on what is within our control, provided that this is meaningful to us, except for power fantasy. Thus, acceptance is the most rational stance. Keeping focus on what is within our control is a key that can change our world and can help us to look and reflect on what is happening and what will happen.

The way we consider and see ourselves as people is also linked to our internal locus of control, what belongs to us is within our control and creates a reorganisation stance. Starting from the limits of what is out with our control leads us back to do the best we can, within the boundaries of our existence. This is a humble stance, be aware of our mortality, of our limitations as human beings, albeit aware of what we can observe. Focus on this foundation of humility and internal control creates motivation and encourages us to re-evaluate our existence. This is a stance close to Seneca, Epictetus, and Marcus Aurelius (Dell'Erba & Nuzzo, 2010; Robertson, 2019; Warburton, 2007).

Our awareness is enhanced by our ability to reflect on what is within our control, redirects us towards gratitude for what we have and what is around us.

On reflection we have a list full of stimuli and opportunities given for granted; to reconsider and re-evaluate them allows us to be grateful.

Gratitude for which is within our control may radically change our life and what we feel about ourselves and others.

It should not be taken for granted that gratitude is linked to the meaning of giving something back, whether symbolic or not, for instance to be kind, smile, help friends and people we do not know. This leaves us open to wonder. A sense of wonder creates an open stance, a thoughtful outlook towards ourselves, others, and the world around us. Gratitude, wonder, awareness, humility, patience, acceptance, focus, enthusiasm; they are all meaningful aspects for whoever is open to a proactive mind.

3.13 The Therapeutic Relationship

The therapeutic relationship has become a common path where several and different psychotherapeutic models engage in exchange of ideas (Safran & Muran, 2000).

Several authors and colleagues (see Gabbard, 2014) consider the importance of the therapeutic relationship as antagonist to evidence-based approaches, such as CBT. It is interesting to note that evidence-based approaches are as such based on recurring aspects of operational modalities, but also on CBT constructs.

It is possible to support each other through modulation of reciprocal relationships, as illustrated by Michael Tomasello (2018).

Such knowledge is empirically supported by Tomasello's research, which has been focused on developmental psychology with emphasis on primates and infants, and lately on adults' relationships. Tomasello outlined the principles of altruism: chimpanzees and human infants' possess the precocious ability to cooperate, even when aware that altruistic actions will not be reciprocated.

Individual support through social motivational systems and different functional emotional systems relationships are supported by other psychotherapy approaches such as Compassion Focus Therapy which is also based on evolutionary theories, and developed by Paul Gilbert, or by Liotti's Cognitive Evolutionary Psychotherapy. These contributions represent a shift from individualistic psychotherapy (Hayes, Hofmann, & Ciarrochi, 2020).

Throughout the history of philosophy and psychology, an outstanding number of methodologies and interventions aimed at supporting and healing psychological suffering, date back to Ancient Greeks, and probably even before them, as discovered by Pierre Hadot (1981, 1995, 2000).

The influence of Pierre Hadot's work is significant in this context, as he revitalised Greek and Roman Philosophy, and in particular Stoicism. Hadot contributed to the renaissance of philosophy, as an applied subject, rather than purely a theoretical and academic discipline.

When psychotherapy started to be formalised as a treatment, from the half of the 19th century (Robertson, 2019), it was already known that certain stances or attitudes towards patients could favourably affect prognosis.

The nature and intent therapeutic relationships to reducing suffering had been considered a crucial part of psychotherapy. Thus, therapeutic relationship was also considered a prerequisite of psychotherapy.

Several theoretical orientations and approaches considered the relationship with patients and clients with different emphases, so that over time, it became evident that the therapeutic relationship was a crucial component, and source of contrast within different therapeutic perspectives.

Psychological research based on evidence-based therapies (Sturmey & Hersen, 2012) led to in depth exploration of the background of therapeutic relationship and its key processes, in such as a way that the Therapeutic Relationship itself can become part of a transtheoretical asset (heritage) and an encounter of clinical researchers (Sturmey & Hersen, 2012).

The core process at the foundation of the therapeutic relationship is the Theory of Mind (ToM), a construct that defines the ability of an individual to sense and to comprehend the mind of another, resulting in mutual understanding (Carcione et al., 2016; Tarricone, 2011).

ToM catalysed the interest of psychology and neuroscience in the last twenty years in quite a formidable way, expanding research databases and developments, as in few other disciplines. Some ToM contributions highlight that there is a difference between comprehending and sensing other person's processes ToM is associated to Meta Cognitive research (Tarricone, 2011), in that ToM is a subset of Metacognitions (i.e. cognitions have the mind, our own mind and the other's mind as a focus).

In this field, different languages have been utilised to capture the most relevant aspects of the Therapeutic Relationship by different authors (Tarricone, 2011). These terms include

- Mentalisation
- Metacognition
- Theory of Mind – ToM
- Metarepresentation
- Self-Reflexivity
- Mindfulness

All of these constructs, which have their own specificity, position the human mind in a place in which it can be observed, understood, identified, perceived, considered, and self-regulated on several core processes. Therefore, from a given point onward it is challenging to focus on the therapeutic relationship without focussing on the parallel interpersonal and metacognitive processes.

In this instance, to comprehend our own mind, and the other's mind, the therapeutic relationship becomes a prerequisite for a constructive interaction that may satisfy mutual goals and objectives and expectations. A compromised therapeutic relationship becomes an ever-emerging focus of study, research, and procedures (Carcione et al., 2016). The tradition to place a strong emphasis on the therapeutic relationship dates back to Freudian

Psychoanalysis, in which transference and countertransference play a key role.

Contemporary psychotherapies are also focused on similar principles, based on each own's appraisal and therapeutic orientation. Few relevant examples are Metacognitive Therapy (Wells, 2008), DBT (Linehan, 1993), ACT (Hayes et al., 2012), SchemaTherapy (Young et al., 2003). Social and Evolutionary Psychology also played a key role in this regard (Hayes & Hofmann, 2018; Hayes et al., 2020).

The Therapeutic relationship is characterised by:

- Interpersonal interactions aimed at decreasing the suffering of one individual, so that he may feel accepted, more confident, more understood and not judged as a person. This lead to restoring the concept that there is a benevolent person with whom we may talk that has a within a safe and contained boundary protected by the nature of relationship
- A second orientation, which is characterised by considering the Therapeutic relationship the main vehicle to appraise, identify and re-evaluate important unresolved conflictual relationships, or dysfunctional ways to pursue individual objectives, which undermine the individual's well-being. Through the Therapeutic Relationship, a person may work on such conflicts and dysfunctional aspects of a relationship to focus on what is important to him. For instance, in a session it may be identified the specific modality of thought and interaction with the other (the therapist in this instance), and develop awareness of the nature of such modality and distance himself from it
- A third orientation consists in considering the Therapeutic Relationship as an alliance, aimed at intervening in situations that may cause distress to an individual, for instance. This alliance is established on the basis of some principles and aspects that reflect the therapist's orientation, but that have common ground that constitute the foundation of the therapeutic relationship.

From a general perspective, the concept of therapeutic relationship has positioned itself over several therapeutic approaches, with some variation in theoretical and technical terminology. Approaches which were entirely different are now linked by a similar way to consider the interaction between therapist and the patient and by key issues at play in the psychotherapeutic session.

An exception lies in Beck's CBT, which has at its core the concept of Collaborative Empiricism, which charts with clarity its boundaries and applications (Beck, 2011). Recent psychotherapy research and meta-analysis concerning the therapeutic relationship indicate that Collaborative Empiricism is supported by evidence (Norcross, 2012).

Of relevance is that the components of Collaborative Empiricism, i.e. adhering to operalisation and verification of hypothesis, mutual collabora- tion, and feedback aimed at collaborative understanding of the individual and his difficulties, may be considered in perspective inspired by therapeutic alliance.

This is a unifying turning point that has had a significant technical impact.

Jeremy Safran and Christopher Muran's work on rupture and repair of Therapeutic Alliance is of considerable significance within the evolution of this concept and has positioned itself as a benchmark for each approach, we refer to this as an "anchor point" (Safran & Muran, 2000).

Safran and Muran updated Strupp, Binder, and Luborsky work (Safran & Muran, 2000), conceptualised within an integrative perspec- tive by Edward Bordin in 1979 (Bordin, 1979). Bordin also considered therapeutic relationships as a prerequisite to therapy. In this instance, we note that the tripartition of Goals-Tasks- Bond, captures factors actively identified interventions in psychotherapy, whilst for Safran and Muran (2000), these factors become independent and active variables in thera- peutic processes.

We may conceptualise at least three approaches within interpersonal modulations of the therapeutic relationship – depending on theoretical perspectives:

- Negotiation, inspired by Safran and Muran (2000). This approach con- siders at its core the identification of triggers of crisis and rupture, or at least of disturbance – upheaval of therapeutic relationship, and the implementation of restorative – repairing interventions, without inter- ference of psychological problems or the therapist
- Psychological re-processing interventions based on identification of dysfunctional, cognitive inflexible modes, dysfunctional coping and relational patterns, are activated in session, in clinical mode (Hayes & Hofmann, 2018). Numerous examples in psychodynamic and cognitive therapy utilise this perspective, with several theoretical and terminolog- ical variations, not always distinct and incompatible (Lemma, Target, & Fonagy, 2011).
- Cooperation. Although this does not seem to greatly differ from the previous aspects, such perspective within the therapeutic relation- ship places a strong emphasis on a joint collaboration between roles in session and directs operations on collaboration in relation to the patient's goals, on what is important to him. This approach is present in third-Wave CBT, and less clearly so in existential psychotherapies centred on life goals and less focused on clinical disorders (Hayes & Hofmann, 2018).

We may see how these approaches co-exist to define specific problems: when is relevant to focus on a specific clinical condition, and in what relational – psychological context.

- These factors linked to these approaches may be:
- Cooperation and mutual respect
- Negotiation and relationship repair
- Analysis and re-processing of psychological patterns in sessions

In clinical settings, these approaches are consistently and flexibly utilised as staple of psychotherapeutic work.

3.14 Therapeutic Setting

We will now focus on a central point of psychotherapy, Setting and Session Structure. This is a compelling aspect, considering all of the different approaches.

There are several considerations on boundaries that make a psychotherapy session possible and that forge the agreements at the core of safety, stabilisation, and containment to psychotherapy processes and contents (Lemma et al., 2011).

Place is crucial. A study, a surgery, a safe room or an online platform are something more than a simple place to meet.

The therapy room has substantial therapeutic potential, compared to a GP surgery or a professional's office. It is the place where an individual should feel safe and protected, knowing that he may disclose his concerns, what he feels, and thinks and talks about what causes suffering for him. In such place a person may express his ideas and feelings within the respect and the safety of a confidential therapeutic relationship.

A place where we may face our fears can be any place. However, a safe, predictable place is recommended so a therapy place becomes evocative in nature, and most importantly, a safe base.

Times are also important (Beck, 2011). Set times are linked to organisational aspects of work, along with dates. Time agreements should always be the same and agreed on both sides, not as an obligation, but because it connotes respect for one another. Third is the clarification regarding the main therapeutic modality, in what it consists, and what are the expectations. Fourth are the boundaries between sessions (Beck, 2011). Regardless of the therapeutic orientation, the psychotherapist and his patients, or clients are not friends. There can be an amicable relationship, and positive feelings towards one another. However, psychotherapy takes priority. Patient's psychological needs may alter the representation that the patient has of his therapist, and such representations might lead to privilege feelings that are less centered on the other, rather than on key figures, towards which the patient or client is interpersonally sensitive.

Conversely, the therapist may also experience blurred emotions- this is the process based on transference and countertransference. The setting and therapeutic boundaries should take into account such significant interpersonal processes. Contact outside session – some approaches set strict boundaries (Beck, 2011; Lemma et al., 2011) in this regard, other approaches are more flexible (Hayes et al., 2012). It all depends on how such interactions (i.e. emails, phone calls, messages) are utilised in therapy.

A session may have a structure in concordance with its approach. Some therapies are very structured in nature, such as CBT; others like ACT are much more flexible. There are no defined standards. It might depend on how the work is organised and how it is planned and prioritised. Structure and orientation may represent an advantage, as proposed by certain evidence-based protocols (Sturmey & Hersen, 2012). However, it may also represent a disadvantage, a price which is too high to pay, and that may negatively affect prognostic outcomes.

Breaking boundary settings should be explored in therapy, as boundaries are an essential requirement for evidence based psychotherapeutic delivery.

Certain setting violations may be damaging towards patients. Others are not therapeutic, but not damaging either. Others, such as sexual relationships and business are forbidden, until there is a therapeutic relationship and no clear ending. This is highlighted in the Codes of Ethics and Conduct of Psychological Society.

Therapy setting is far more than a series of bullet points to agree upon, it represents a mental structure that creates a boundary to the patient and therapist's own fantasies (Lemma et al., 2011).

A session might be characterised by many tactical and strategic levels, and usually intense; what is said and not said does not exhaust what characterises sessions. A session may incorporate several aspects. Usually, patients would like to discuss some difficulties while the therapist also has his own agenda. Silence and what is not communicated might also represent a crucial session focus (Beck, 2011; Lemma et al., 2011).

There is usually a list of the difficulties experienced by the patient or client; this may depend on therapy orientation. These problems can be reformulated within a psychological model that, although trans-theoretical, is affected by the clinical-theoretical approach.

The therapist should consider different factors, often simultaneously. Setting and boundaries are one of these, as well as the diagnosis and its implication in terms of psychological suffering.

The patients or clients' mental state at a given moment in session, might represent another relevant factor to consider. We assume that the focus is on what was brought by the patient in session (Carcione et al., 2016; Young et al., 2003).

Different CBT approaches denote sessions by reflecting on salient points. However, the common denominator is the transformative aspect of the patient's perspective, and all that is required to facilitate work in this profession.

3.15 Case Example

Victoria was a 39-year-old lawyer, married to Giulio, a 44-year-old nurse.

Victoria's parents died in a car crash when she was 14 years old. She lived with her brother (now married and high school teacher) and moved in with their grandparents. Victoria's grandparents died, due to cancer and cardiac problems.

Victoria went to her GP due to insomnia and gastric problems. Her GP subsequently referred her to a community mental health service.

Victoria was seen by one of the authors (GLD), with whom she started psychotherapy for mild depression and Narcissistic personality traits.

Victoria's difficulties were centered around interpersonal relationships; she felt disrespected and experienced subsequent anger and hostile ruminative, apparently depressed mood and affect, whenever she was in an argument.

As psychotherapeutic work progressed, Victoria identified schemas linked to Defectiveness and Abandonment, which were linked to her life experience, after her parents' death and moving to live with her grandparents.

Victoria processed these memories in session, and challenged those feelings, managing to differentiate them, thus recalibrating them within the present moment in session.

Collaborative formulation of the past and present perspectives represented a turning point, which resulted in Victoria's increased ability to understand herself and to realistically appraise her feelings. Victoria genuinely processed her parents' loss for the first time.

References

Alford, B., & Beck, A.T. (1997). *The integrative power of cognitive therapy*. New York, NY: Guilford Press.
Allen, J.G., Fonagy, P., & Bateman, A.W. (2008). *Mentalization in clinical practice*. Washington, DC: American Psychiatric Publishing.
American Psychiatric Association. (2012). *Diagnostic and statistical manual of mental disorders (DSM 5)* (5th ed.). Washington, DC: APA.
Arntz, A., & Lobbestael, J. (2018). Cognitive structures and processes in personality disorders. In W.J. Livesley & R. Larstone (Eds.), *Handbook of personality disorders: Theory, research, and treatment* (pp. 141–154). New York, NY: Guilford Press.

Baer, R. (2018). *Mindfulness practice*. In S.C. Hayes & S.G. Hofmann (Eds.), *Process based CBT*. Oakland, CA: Content Press/New Harbinger.

Barlow D. H. (2010). Negative effects from psychological treatments: A perspective. *The American psychologist*, *65*(1), 13–20. https://doi.org/10.1037/a0015643

Barlow, D.H., Allen, L.B., & Choate, M.L. (2004). Toward a unified treatment for emotional disorders. *Behavior Therapy*, *35*, 205–230.

Barlow, D.H., Sauer-Zavala, S., Carl, J.R., Bullis, J.R., & Ellard, K.K. (2014). The nature, diagnosis, and treatment of neuroticism: Back to the future. *Clinical Psychological Science*, *2*(3), 344–365.

Beck, A.T. (1967). *Depression: Clinical, experimental, and theoretical aspects*. Philadelphia: University of Pennsylvania Press.

Beck, A.T., Rector, N.A., Stolar, N., & Grant, P. (2008). *Schizophrenia: Cognitive theory, research, and therapy*. New York, NY: Guilford Press.

Beck, J.S. (2011). *Cognitive behavior therapy: Basics and beyond*. New York, NY: Guilford Press.

Bentall, R. (2009). *Doctoring the mind: Is our current treatment of mental illness really any good?* New York, NY: New York University Press.

Bordin, E.S. (1979). The generalizability of the psychoanalytic concept of the working alliance. *Psychotherapy: Theory, Research & Practice*, *16*(3), 252–260.

Carcione, A., Niccolò, G., & Semerari, A. (2016). *Curare i casi complessi*. Bari-Roma: Laterza.

Cupitt, C. (2019). *CBT for psychosis: Process-orientated therapies and the third wave*. New York, NY: Routledge.

Dahl, J., Plumb, J.C., Stewart, I., & Lundgren, T. (2009). *The art and science of valuing in psychotherapy. Helping clients discover, explore, and commit to valued action using acceptance and commitment therapy*. Oakland, CA: New Harbinger.

Davidson, D. (1987). *Subjective, intersubjective, objective*. Oxford: Oxford University Press.

Dell'Erba, G.L., Carati, M.A., Greco, S., & Muya, M. (2009). *La sindrome ansiosa*. Milano: Franco Angeli.

Dell'Erba, G.L., & Nuzzo, E. (2010). *Psicologia pratica*. Lecce: Pensa Editore.

Dobson, K. (2010). *Handbook of cognitive behavior therapy*. New York, NY: Guilford Press.

Fennell, M. (1997). Low self-esteem: A cognitive perspective. *Behavioural and Cognitive Psychotherapy*, *25*(1), 1–26. doi:10.1017/S1352465800015368

Gabbard, G.O. (2014). *Psychodynamic psychiatry in clinical practice*. Arlington, VA: American Psychiatric Publishing.

Gabbard, G.O. (2015). *Psychodynamic psychiatry in clinical practice* (4th ed.). Arlington, VA: American Psychiatric Publishing.

Gilbert, P. (2014). The origins and nature of compassion focused therapy. *British Journal of Clinical Psychology*, *79*(5), 618–628.

Goleman, D. (1997). *Emotional intelligence: Why it can matter more than IQ*. New York City, NY: Bantam Books.

Hadot, P. (1981). *Esercizi spirituali e filosofia antica*. Torino: Einaudi.

Hadot, P. (1995). *Philosophy as a way of life: Spiritual exercises from Socrates to Foucault* (with J. Carlier and A. I. Davidson). Blackwell.

Hadot, P. (2000). (contributor). *Manuale di Epitteto*. Torino: Einaudi..

Hayes, S.C. (2019). Acceptance and commitment therapy: Towards a unified model of behavior change. *World Psychiatry*, *18*(2), 226–227. doi:10.1002/wps.20626

Hayes, S.C., & Hofmann, S.G. (2018). *Process based CBT*. Oakland, CA: Content Press/New Harbinger.

Hayes, S.C., Hofmann, S.G., & Ciarrochi, J. (2020). A process-based approach to psychological diagnosis and treatment: The conceptual and treatment utility of an extended evolutionary model. *Clinical Psychology Review*, *82*, 101908. doi:10.1016/j. cpr.2020.101908

Hayes, S.C., Levin, M.E., Plumb-Vilardaga, J, Villatte, J.L., & Pistorello, J. (2013). Acceptance and commitment therapy and contextual behavioral science: examining the progress of a distinctive model of behavioral and cognitive therapy. *Behaviour Therapy*, *44*(2):180–198. doi: 10.1016/j.beth.2009.08.002.

Hayes, S.C., Strosahal, K.D., & Wilson, K.G. (2012). *Acceptance and commitment therapy*. New York, NY: Guilford Press.

Johnson-Laird, P.N., Mancini, F., & Gangemi, A. (2006). A hyperemotion theory of psychological illnesses. *Psychological Review*, *113*(4), 822–841.

Legrenzi, P. (2019). *Storia della psicologia* (6th ed.). Bologna: Il Mulino.

Lemma, A., Target, M., & Fonagy, P. (2011). *Brief dynamic interpersonal therapy: A clinician's guide*. Oxford: Oxford University Press.

Linehan, M. (1993). *Cognitive-behavioral treatment of borderline personality disorder*. New York, NY: Guilford Press.

Lysaker, P.H., & Klion, R.E. (2018). *Recovery: Meaning-making and severe mental illness. A comprehensive guide to metacognitive reflection an insight therapy*. London: Routledge.

Mele, A. (2001). *Self-deception unmasked*. Princeton, NJ: Princeton University Press.

Miceli, M., & Castelfranchi, C. (2014). *Expectancy and emotion*. Oxford: Oxford University Press.

Norcross, J. (2012). *Psychotherapy relationships that work* (2nd ed.). New York, NY: American Psychological Association.

Pedrini, P. (2019). Unconceptualized internal promptings: Methodological pluralism and the new cartography of the mind. *Philosophia*, *47*, 303–312.

Premack, D., & Premack, J. (1983). *The mind of an ape*. New York, NY: Norton.

Robertson, D. (2019). *The philosophy of cognitive-behavioural therapy (CBT)*. London: Routledge.

Safran, J.D., & Muran, J.C. (2000). Resolving therapeutic alliance ruptures: Diversity and integration. *Journal of Clinical Psychology*, *56*(2), 233–243.

Seligman, M.E.P. (1990). *Learned optimism*. New York, NY: Knopf.

Smith, E., & Bem, D.J. & Nolen-Hoeksema, S. (2004). *Fundamentals of psychology*. San Diego, CA: Harcourt.

Sturmey, P., & Hersen, M. (2012). *Handbook of evidence based practice in clinical psychology*. Hoboken, NJ: Wiley.

Tarricone, P. (2011). *The taxonomy of metacognition*. East Sussex: Psychology Press.

Taylor, S.E. (1989). *Positive illusions: Creative self-deception and the healthy mind*. New York, NY, Basic Books/Hachette Book Group.

Tomasello, M. (2018). *A natural history of human thinking*. Cambridge, MA: Harvard University Press.

Warburton, N. (2007). *Philosophy: The basics*. London: Routledge.

Wegner, D.M., & Schneider, D.J. (2003). The white bear story. *Psychological Inquiry*, *14*(3/4), 326–329. http://www.jstor.org/stable/1449696

Wegner, D.M., Schneider, D.J., Carter, S.R., III, & White, T.L. (1987). Paradoxical effects of thought suppression. *Journal of Personality and Social Psychology*, *53*(1), 5–13.

Wells, A. (1997). *Cognitive therapy of anxiety disorders: A practice manual and conceptual guide*. Chichester: Wiley.

Wells, A. (2009). *Metacognitive therapy for anxiety and depression*. New York, NY: Guilford Press.

Wells, A. (2011). *Metacognitive therapy for anxiety and depression*. New York, NY: Guilford Press.

Young, J., Klosko, J.S., & Weishaar, M.E. (2003). *Schema therapy. A practitioner's guide*. New York, NY: Guilford Press.

Chapter 4

Challenges Posed by Complexity

4.1 Resistance

We often wonder in what way we can facilitate therapy, or how we may decrease our patients' difficulties in practising what they learned in therapy. In this particular instance, may there be a specific challenge or experience that might adversely impact on treatment objectives and goals? We define this as resistance; but what is resistance, exactly?

The concept of resistance originated from Freudian Psychoanalysis. This directs our attention towards the patient's unconscious attempts to protect the meaning and functional aspects of their symptoms, which can be considered aggressive, intrusive, and intolerable (Legrenzi, 2019; Smith, Bem, & Nolen-Hoeksema, 2004).

The meaning that psychotherapists attribute to patients' resistance is significantly influenced by two main factors, currently.

The first one is the collaboration between the patient and the therapist; its foundation lies on the psychological processes that underpin the therapeutic relationship. Collaboration and a sound therapeutic alliance are centred around mutual therapy goals and the means utilised to pursue such goals, i.e. reciprocal respect and bond (Bordin, 1979).

In this context, ruptures of the therapeutic relationship are part of active therapeutic work, and we believe they may be reasonably attributed to resistance (Safran & Muran, 2000). An ulterior factor is the attribution and meaning of control. Control is characterised by two main components (Seligman, 1991):

- External, thus individuals assume a passive stance
- Internal, thus individuals attribute themselves power and control over events

Following such logic, a psychotherapist may feel omnipotent, and subsequently disappointed, or confused by resistance. Conversely, a psychotherapist may feel out of control, therefore attributing resistance to the patient.

DOI: 10.4324/9781003299226-5

These factors are pivotal in psychotherapy and within the therapeutic relationship. We believe that the concept of therapeutic relationship is invaluable and stimulating for the reflection and collaboration between the patient and the psychotherapist.

Let's briefly reconsider resistance as initially defined by psychoanalysis. A psychotherapist allies himself or herself with the patient who is suffering, and they work together to unhinge entrenched stumbling blocks and reframe our wild, "reptilian" tendencies (sex and aggression).

Patients and clients may be considered allies and antagonists (Lemma, Target, & Fonagy, 2011; Safran & Muran, 2000). Such consideration follows current requirements to work with patients, to build self-awareness and address on meta-cognitions, along with patients' and clients' abilities to be aware of their own psychological processes, how they make sense to them, and how to accept them by understanding, thus realistically changing their goals and valued sense of direction.

Mutual understanding may also mean the identification and conceptualisation of certain behaviours and strategies as understandable within previous experiences and that had been appraised as painful. This process may be complex in nature. We all have our own idea of ourselves, and it may be painful to explore, should this process lead to experiencing emotional pain; self-deception and resistance closely follow this process.

Current psychotherapeutic perspectives (Norcross, 2012; Safran & Muran, 2000) consist in comprehending resistance within therapy, therapy being considered by patients and clients as foreboding of emotional suffering, at least at the beginning of therapy.

Patients embark in life and cope with frustration and adversities, by building coping strategies, which will become inflexible and stereotyped in nature and therefore dysfunctional. However, such coping strategies are subjective answers to suffering and personal experiences that caused trauma, frustrations, and left anything that was perceived as being unsustainable. Such emotional pain is a construct which is superimposable to cognitive interpersonal schemas (its reverse aspects are captured by Bowlby's internal models) (Lemma et al., 2011). Thus, resistance is a coping strategy in therapy, which protects the patient from the pain of facing or exploring a painful psychological issue with his psychotherapist.

Resistance may be linked to transference and to interpersonal schemas, as also in keeping with most contemporary cognitive psychotherapies (Lemma et al., 2011; Safran & Muran, 2000). Negative interpersonal schemas, dysfunctional coping strategies, identification and co-construction of meaning, and understanding of patterns within a patient's own history act in session as mental states synchronous with coping strategies; these are all processes that are common to psychodynamic psychotherapy and cognitive therapies.

4.2 Iatrogenic Psychotherapy

It is worthwhile considering whether psychotherapy may be iatrogenic, when considering efficacy and effectiveness of treatments.

Psychotherapy may not be effective, in that clinical conditions may not improve; this results in disappointment, whenever this is the case; however, at least it is not detrimental to mental health. Conversely, iatrogenic treatments are likely to cause psychological problems.

Some theories may directly or indirectly contribute to supporting irrational and dysfunctional assumptions. These assumptions are often inherent to behaviours, which denote presentation of individuals who suffer from anxiety, personality disorders, and depression.

Statements related to questionable or disreputable treatments are as follows:

1 Release – get rid of anger
2 Distraction from negative emotions or thoughts
3 Depression equals self-punishment
4 Believe in something due to self-interest
5 If I think something, it must be true
6 Intense emotions are damaging or dangerous
7 Emotions express what is true
8 Individuals have choices and responsibility for their own actions, or no choices and responsibility
9 Self-esteem must be enhanced. Improving self-esteem
10 Frustration must be avoided or managed

Although these statements appear inspiring in nature, they often lead to damaging behaviours.

Each one of these statements is linked to a complex matrix of statements particularly dysfunctional in its essence.

1 Getting rid of anger is characterised by two main problems in psychology. One is related to the old and problematic concept of "elimination." Eliminating an emotion means to metaphorically modify our being. Furthermore, getting rid of something means to release or to expel. There is nothing equivalent to this action in psychology (i.e. concepts of catharsis). The release of emotions or urges is found in Freud (Smith et al., 2004), and in early psychology and philosophy, which theorised "mental energy" (Robertson, 2019). Further concerns related to "energy release" stemming from emotions are to define emotions as targets to eliminate, as long as we can achieve a peaceful state of mind

A mental state void of emotions may be achievable through meditation; however, it is not desirable for our lives, at least in the way we conceive them. It is as if we have to experience positive feelings, whereby other feelings become "abnormal" and have to be managed, or eliminated.

It has been demonstrated that attempts to manage and oppose feelings worsen our emotional states and lead to further psychological problems (Legrenzi, 2019). Contemporary psychology perspectives on emotions are not usually considered in this kind of "energy theories" (Smith et al., 2004).

2 Distraction, i.e. focus our attention elsewhere to avoid unwanted thoughts and emotions, is the focus of several well-known research studies (Wegner, 1989). Intrusive thoughts and emotions may be hindered or managed at a cost, that is the worsening of our mental health or psychological problems. There are several research studies that focus on the paradoxical effects of thought suppression (Hayes & Hofmann, 2018; Wegner, 1989), which prove the pejorative effect of avoidance strategies, including distraction on our mind. Undesired stimuli re-occur further in an effort to suppress them. Thus, any psychotherapeutic technique that focuses on control or avoidance of intrusive cognitions and emotions will cause a clinical deterioration in patients' mental state. We note that there are several theoretical models that actively prescribe control and avoidance techniques (Dobson, 2010), despite the fact that they are not recommended

3 Depression equals self-punishment: this is dated Freudian concept, which led, amongst other things, to the development of Beck's Cognitive Therapy. Beck evidenced that depressive states are originated by beliefs linked to loss and self-criticism and are certainly not driven by self-punishment (Beck, 2011). This is linked to the psychologist's fallacy, i.e. the confusion between the psychologist's perspective and the mental experience that is being reported. Self-criticism and meaning attributed to loss determine emotional states linked to sadness, and perpetuating factors maintain a depressive cycle. Self-punishment hardly causes depression, but other complex emotions, linked to impulsivity and dysregulation

4 Believe in something due to self-interest – a belief is determined by evidence that is considered to be plausible by individuals (Miceli & Castelfranchi, 2014). Thus, we tend to believe due to plausibility. A belief may have unintended consequences, as beliefs often come at a cost. However, the cost of believing in something is not linked to its content. For instance, if I believe that I cannot afford grapes, this has a cost, i.e. grapes in themselves that are not within my reach and related upset are different in nature. Each attempt to modify the content of my beliefs on grapes, i.e. it might be unripe, it is unripe, and I have lost nothing, has elevated psychological costs. Thus, the analysis of believing in something due to self-interest leads to a perilous path, which should always be discouraged. Sartre referred to this notion as bad faith (Sartre, 2003)

5   If I think something, it must be true. It is a classic cognitive shortcut that comes at a cost. It is the symbol of an egocentric and naïve modality at cognitive level. Piaget described this process at length in his theories of cognitive development (Smith et al., 2004). Cognitive therapy (Beck, 2011; Wells, 1997) incorporated this concept amongst the main dysfunctional cognitive processes in Emotional Disorders. Here it emerges from the construct of intrusive thought; its interpretation stemming as a stimulus from (external reality), not as mental process, determines between mind and reality. Any attempt to legitimise an intrusive thought as a foreboding of external information is unsound. Furthermore, this kind of perspective conveys naïve minds, and almost as pathological as the one that is presumed as experienced by the patient

6   Intense emotions are damaging or dangerous. It is certainly a classic therapeutic step when working with patients who suffer from anxiety. The most galvanising aspect is that such an erroneous and dysfunctional stance is shared amongst most professionals, including psychotherapists (Dell'Erba et al., 2009). Several years ago, these authors conducted a research study on beliefs related to damage caused by anxiety; results indicated that patients suffering from anxiety experienced the highest degree of beliefs regarding dangerous emotions. An unpublished result is that doctors, nurses, and social workers also presented with an elevated degree of belief in this regard, although not as elevated as patients. This may lead us to believe that our beliefs can drive iatrogenic interventions through erroneous and dysfunctional beliefs (Dell'Erba et al., 2009)

7   Emotions express truth, or emotions provide information on reality. These are naïve perspectives that are linked to what has been discussed so far. Emotions are regulated by cognitions, which establish the meaning of a stimulus or a situation. Thus, emotions are subsequent or secondary to cognitions (Dobson, 2010; Miceli & Castelfranchi, 2014). Their nature of involuntary, sudden mental states makes it difficult to recognise and differentiate them from a psychological perspective: emotions appear as primary and not as a result of judgements. Hence, considering emotional states as information on reality or on what seems to be genuine and authentic is an outdated ideological trap (Smith et al., 2004). If anxiety conveyed information of what is real on this planet, we would already be extinct. Furthermore, if emotions lost their nature as information on changes in relationships between individuals and contexts, we would probably be extinct, even if they were not easily discernible by individuals

8   Most psychotherapeutic perspectives focus on what is within our control and responsibility. This is a key aspect of a person's mental health and psychological well-being. However, some psychological

perspectives focus this issue in a dichotomous and polarised stance. Some models tend to consider patients or people as equipped with enormous power and control, and thus able to influence a wide range of their lives (Dobson, 2010). Conversely, other theoretical models, like the phenomenological and psychoanalytic approaches during the 40s and 50s (Legrenzi, 2019) consider our psychological lives determined by aspects or factors from the past, or external to our lives and therefore factors that we are unaware of and cannot control. Contemporary psychology examines the process of choice and decision, as key factors for our psychological well-being and quality of life. Some factors may re-calibrate the unknown nature of most of these evaluative decision-making processes and therefore contribute to creating favourable conditions to conscious choices, whilst considering advantages and disadvantages. One of the factors that increase our ability to make these decisions is our psychological competencies, or metacognitions

9 Improving self-esteem. This is a popular trend that considers self-esteem as "reified," as it were an organ of our body. Self-esteem narratives become similar to dysfunctional or malfunctioning mechanisms, as if we are referring to a device. The term self-esteem may be linked to the unfortunate propensity to evaluate the performance of an individual as his own worth as a human being, with disastrous consequences. In such instances, it might become a psychological trap and morph into a prejudice against us. Improving self-esteem does not always lead to desired benefits. This message carries a covert connotation: my worth as a human being can be measured, a perilous path indeed

10 Frustration must be avoided or managed. This is a classical Stoic theme (Robertson, 2019), but a contemporary one also. Acceptance and openness are influential concepts, at the core of several theoretical psychotherapeutic systems, such as S. Hayes's ACT (2012). Accepting and being open to our emotions and to NOs that we can receive from several contexts is crucial. Trying to manage or to override emotional consequences of the NOs is bound to fail. As previously discussed, "emotions management techniques" (Wegner, 1989) lead to disadvantages that outweigh the problem itself. Furthermore, frustration provides us with important information regarding our own limitations as human beings, in relation to specific contexts and goals. Thus, if frustration is interpreted as negative, or as an incongruous fault of our Psychological or Biological selves, we would lose our ability to discern between fantasy and reality. We would not be cognisant of what we can or cannot control. This is the well-known Stoic Fork, the incipit of Epictetus' Manual (Hadot, 2000): ENCHIRIDION of Epictetus, and consists of the key sayings of the famous Stoic teacher Epictetus

Therefore, attempts to manage, control, avoid, and combat frustration, rather than accepting it as a source of learning and information, lead to worsening of quality of life, tranquillity, and ability to pursue our goals.

To conclude, these considerations signpost therapies that at their best do not support patients and/or clients to understand what is important to them and, at their worst, worsen their difficulties. In other words, these considerations identify harmful and iatrogenic psychotherapies.

4.3 Conflict

Arbitrary beliefs, such as negative cognitive schemas, or sweeping generalisations, such as catastrophising, extreme and unrealistic pessimism, inflexible self-blame, and entitlement, may contribute or exacerbate psychological suffering, thus causing harm. Moreover, they might pose an obstacle to change or improvement and to lead a life that is objectively and/or subjectively meaningful.

Human beings pursue multiple goals and hold a multitude of beliefs on themselves (according to Beck, 1975) or beliefs as to how things should be (according to Ellis, 1994) and on what is or is not normal (according to Wells, 2008), and on as to whether we are more or less aware of our interpersonal stances (according to Young, Klosko, & Weishaar, 2003). But there is something more; it is possible to coherently describe this process in keeping with conflict, thus pertinent to the patient's goals and motivation.

Motivation is linked to pursuit of goals; thus it may also regulate behaviours. Not all goals are driven by the same motivation, and not all of them are relevant and simultaneously active. Some goals can be intertwined with other goals, thus creating conflict. Goals' conflict is part of complex systems and is regulated by procedures focused on problem-solving and choosing goals. When goals are incongruous with each other, they are evaluated against several features, including being useful and functional, and support other fundamental/primary goals relevant to individuals. A goal has value, as it is important to achieve another goal.

Sometimes choices appear immediate and influenced by unconscious actions. Emotions can also compromise or threaten the pursuit of goals. For instance, choosing between two actions, whereby the first action is less anxiety provoking than the second. Thus, the first action is less threatening and therefore associated to a lesser extent as a threat to the pursuit of other goals. We may not be fully aware of such an action plan.

When we encounter a conflict between goals, or an internal psychological conflict, we become stuck. Attempting to pursue two opposite goals, or an unachievable goal, becomes frustrating: poor emotional recognition of frustration in this instance, thus normalising erroneous choices or conflict, leads to psychological suffering. Conflict is characterised by two main features and related perspectives (Castelfranchi, Mancini, & Miceli, 2002):

- Challenges posed by choices within a certain perspective
- Irreconcilable goals and the meaning attributed by the individual

From this perspective, conflict may represent an experiential problem. The evaluation of irreconcilable goals constitutes a secondary problem, which has negative connotations.

In primary problems, dichotomous choices are driven by the complex nature of the context, and by human experience. The required exemplification of the evaluation, in a given context, polarises goals and positions individuals in choice and action mode. If we consider polarisation as part of a cognitive emergency process, we may comprehend the motivation to simplify and act and be justified by evolutionary processes.

Naturally, not all context and choices are driven by emergencies, or fight for survival. This is the case when integration of incongruous and conflictual choices can be merged by individuals, from a wider perspective, which may not be immediately evident when we act in emergency contexts.

There is a fundamental distinction at the core of the experience to be in or to deal with conflicts: their identification (Mancini & Giacomantonio, 2018). Identifying the parts of a conflict, and the nature of their psychological components, is a fundamental ability that may make the difference between who can overcome or accept conflict; who does not have such ability might therefore tend to be predisposed to increased emotional and psychological suffering.

A further difference is the perspective involved in the identification of the parts initially in conflict.

A third distinction is the resolution of the conflict. Some goals, if pursued, lead us to frustration or to freeze mode: goals seem to be within our control; however, they are not.

Below there are some examples of unachievable or conflicting goals. These date back to approximately twenty years ago, when Dell'Erba attempted to formalise problems present in several psychopathologies (Dell'Erba, 1998).

1 "I want X and cannot obtain it." This is a conflict between a target and its achievement, which tends to lock individuals between two different negative mental states; one of them is, however, functional. A person may back out and reject his final goal (functional negative state), or he may not renounce and be stuck (negative dysfunctional state). In some instances, such person may not be able to make sense of the situation in which he cannot obtain what he wants, despite desiring it. The person therefore suffers due to this conflict itself. Conflict focuses shifts from "I want X, whilst meaning I am entitled to X"

2   "I want X and Y and I cannot obtain them at the same time." This
    occurs when a person is unable or does not want to make a choice. In
    this scenario, the person does not want to lose. These are pertinent
    unachievable goals or intents and therefore should be considered if
    two goals are incompatible, although a person may want to choose to
    pursue X and then Y. Or the person in question is stuck and therefore
    cannot prioritise and evaluate his goals. It is important to note that "I
    cannot have X and Y" is not accepted and thwarted
3   "I do not want to feel X." This is a choice that revolves on certain con-
    sequences. X out with the individual's direct and intentional control.
    It is impossible to try and directly determine an emotion, for instance.
    Similarly, believing Y and subsequently feeling X is also impossible.
    However, undertaking the strategy of avoiding feeling X is at the core of
    numerous dysfunctional and disastrous strategies that lead to psycho-
    logical suffering and are associated with elevated psychological costs
4   "I want X, but what I should want is Y." Human beings apply different
    criteria in this context. On one hand, we desire X, as it has certain con-
    sequences. On the other hand, we apply different criteria to evaluate
    advantages associated with X. However, as human beings we do not
    fully agree with this rule. This is a classic desire-duty conflict, where
    people do not want to sacrifice or renounce any of the advantages of X
    or Y. Such mental state determines two negative effects: one associated
    with perturbing the pursuit of X; the other associated with self-criticism
    or preoccupation with being criticised for missing Y
5   "I want X, even if I cannot have X." In this instance, even if a person
    believes that his actions will have negative and invalidating repercus-
    sions, he may persist, even when confronted with the glaring evidence
    that he will not be able to obtain X. We might hypothesise that this kind
    of individual may ignore the result, even if complex and multifaceted
    of his own actions, or he does not wish to determine the impact of his
    actions and continues, as a "matter of principle" to focus on such direc-
    tion. We might also consider that an individual may not have any other
    choices; however, there are reasons as to why a person persists, i.e. irra-
    tional hopes. This frame of mind is associated with intransigent behav-
    iours. The focus is on "I want X" meaning "I am entitled to X." This
    should not be confused with "X is" and "X should be." For instance, a
    person believes that an event is unfair, as it goes against a moral rule,
    even when the event is a flood or an earthquake. This represents a dys-
    functional assumption, rather than a conflict
6   "I cannot give up on X. X is everything, an indispensable, absolute need."
    Indispensable matters, to which human beings find no alternative, or to
    which they are not ready to consider an alternative. Often we hold general
    beliefs; some other times they have specific beliefs, which they developed

through certain experiences. Such evaluations and inferences result in beliefs that these expectations constitute the only possible aspect of reality. We may also infer that a person considers an alternative to an absolute need, a catastrophic one at that. Decisions and choices that present a cost in terms of humiliation, guilt, unbearable emotional states, and distress that cannot be tolerated and are linked to Core Beliefs

7 "I do not want to be X": we set ourselves the goal to be different without considering that when we describe ourselves, we do so through other people's judgement, which we covet. This is the so-called Stendhal effect. Such descriptions are not within our control but may only be received as a result of interactions, which may also be out of our control – for instance, our reputation

8 "I do not want to believe X." This is based on the assumption that beliefs are not intentional and therefore may not be chosen. However, patients or clients dispute the nature of several beliefs, based on consequences that such beliefs would cause in terms of advantages or rules based on evaluation, i.e. if I believe in equality, I am a good person. This can lead to self-deception. Some authors, mainly from psychodynamic approaches like Weiss (1990), consider self-deception not as unintentional, but as an attempt to interfere and redirect attention to more neutral cognitive processes. "I want to believe Y. However, wanting to believe Y is different from I wish that Y represents hope or that it might come true"

9 "I do not want S to become X." We tend to believe that we may influence a person's processes. A person wishes that another peer may be in a certain way or may experience certain mental states (or not). A person who believes that X is possible therefore develops a plan to create X, by persisting and apportioning guilt or blame. These kinds of behaviours stem from limited mentalising ability

10 "I do not want Ys to believe X." This represents one of the most significant interpersonal conflicts, and the foundation of most phobias, interpersonal dependence, subjugation, and subordination. It also is one of the most important interventions devised by Albert Ellis (1994) in the Rational Emotive Behaviour Therapy (REBT). Human beings mistake the wish (within our power) for a favourable evaluation, for the pretension (out with our power) of a favourable evaluation. Such consideration may be applied within any interpersonal interaction, where boundaries and individual limitations are blurred. Although we may wish favourable feedback, we might not expect it. We may do anything within our power that might indirectly result in positive feedback, i.e. behave in a benevolent way, be generous, and be kind, but ultimately the outcome is not predictable, as our behaviour does not influence other people's opinions directly. The intent to directly pursue such goals can only result in suffering and deal with personal and interpersonal consequences

4.4 Primary and Secondary Psychological Problems

We often manufacture our own mental traps. Our understanding of what is happening around us and our mental states strongly influences our actions. What can we do to support people to free themselves from psychological traps?

Human beings apply their own knowledge and schemas to what they face, experience, or learn; some of this knowledge and related psychological processes are part of ourselves. We are all predisposed to deal with hypothetical threats, in a certain way, for instance, by being hypervigilant of dangerous stimuli, including our neurophysiological responses (flight, fight, and freeze). Furthermore, each person has his own way of learning, and this categorises certain contexts and stimuli; for instance, certain things are dangerous; other things are unreliable and so forth.

This is a pivotal component required when coping with frustrations or anticipating problems. We also differentiate between problems within ourselves and the external world.

Thus, a fundamental problem in the development of psychological traps is posed by the inability to discern between ourselves and the external world (Robertson, 2019).

A psychological problem is conceptualised differently from diagnostic categories and mental illness. This results in analysing and sharing a patient's perspective and identifying a fear, therefore giving us access to a cognitive and motivational approach.

Psychological problems can be classified as follows:

- Worries
- Lack of motivation
- Losses
- Low self-esteem
- Problem-solving
- Self-realisation
- Disorientation
- Conflict
- Injustice

These are all psychological problems that may be addressed in psychotherapy. However, problems may be primary or secondary; they may be generated due to the fact that we have problems, or due to a particular aspect of such problems. We try to make sense of what happens to us, with the resources we have available.

We may encounter a problem, which might result in intended or unintended consequences – ABC. Our emotional state may become a subsequent problem; consequences may be evaluated negatively, resulting in a secondary subsequent ABC, which in turn subsequently results in a different emotional state (a tertiary ABC).

We are therefore torn between three different mental states, fluctuating between them and appraisals of related content and processes. This may lead to the development of a further mental state based on negative evaluation, which is likely to be associated with emotional dysregulation.

Where is the trap? We cannot disentangle ourselves between those different mental states, as we do not have a "psychological map." Escaping these traps requires psychological competencies. It is worth noticing that there is a constant factor within the dynamic of secondary psychological processes and vicious circles. There is a blueprint that emerges amongst infinite variations and differences:

- A primary problem may be related to any event or fact
- A secondary psychological process may be related to emotional and cognitive processes pertinent to brain and mind functioning
- A tertiary psychological problem is pertinent to self-evaluation and often inherent to our own coping strategies
- A further psychological problem may be related to our self-evaluation, and the root origin of such problems

We have offered a dynamic conceptualisation amongst psychological problems that can slightly vary but maintain the same structure (Hayes & Hofmann, 2018).

We might escape those traps by developing an integrative version of these aspects, noticing them and evaluating them as part of our normal psychological life. What is the most common secondary problem by far? Experiencing pain and not wishing to experience pain or being afraid of experiencing pain.

Self-appraisal of our mental states may lead to unpleasant outcomes; when faced by choices such as trying to attempt and avoiding our emotions, we might develop further psychological problems. This is the most common psychological dilemma by far. We may add that Cognitive Behavioural Therapy (CBT) offers a clear answer to this kind of dilemma.

When patients or clients request a change or psychotherapy, they often ask if they can no longer feel in a certain way, and not to experience certain emotional states. We note that often this should not be taken literally, considering that a person is seeking help to identify the root cause, source of psychological suffering, and cope with it. Sometimes the request is factual, and sadly there is always someone who indulges in this request; we are referring to iatrogenic psychotherapy in this instance.

Often patients struggle to verbalise and clearly describe their difficulties, as they can often rapidly move from one problem to the other. What can we do in this regard and why do we refer to this as "primary and secondary problems"?

A main CBT feature is the identification and conceptualisation of secondary problems (Beck, 2011; Dobson, 2010; Ellis, 1994). Secondary problems are psychological difficulties that stem from consequences of primary psychological issues.

We can utilise ABC model as a tool:

1 To define psychological problems, which can be primary or directed towards the outside world
2 A secondary problem that can have as an Antecedent any aspects of the primary problem

Secondary ABCs are mainly concerned with interpretation of emotions, consequences of primary problems, or mental states that are based on the primary problem.

We can classify secondary problems as follows:

• Type one, in which A is concerned with an emotion, or a mental process such as attention, concentration, memory, or intrusive thought. These As are rooted within the primary problem and are reappraised, thus becoming a new psychological problem
• Type two is a self-critical thought, or a judgement related to our own mental states, as disconnected from the context where they usually occur, for instance, evaluation of coping strategies related to negative themes, or context conceptualised as negative
• Type three constitutes a category of psychological problems related to self-judgement in relation to past experiences, or a judgement on our past tout court, meaning that patients judge themselves as a "standalone effect," and within a bias regarding their own self as a person

Not always secondary problems are experimented with or activated in such a sequence; often the activation of one of them may trigger other ones. It is still not clear as to whether one of these specific secondary problems is intrinsic to a specific psychopathological feature, or associated with a given diagnosis (Hayes, Hofmann, & Ciarocchi, 2020).

Anxious patients often activate secondary problems, which have emotional reactions as content, and the manifestations of such emotions (Beck, 2011). This may also occur in other clinical conditions, such as depression or emotional dysregulation related to personality disorders.

Personality disorders are distinguished by alternating mental states related to coping strategies and concerning interpersonal relationships or stressful situations; this may influence therapeutic focus more directly than in other clinical conditions (Carcione, Niccolò, & Semerari, 2016).

Identification of secondary problems may offer a considerable advantage and accuracy in psychotherapeutic interventions and better elucidates the kind of difficulties that often patients and clients have in recounting their own negative experiences.

A main feature of contemporary CBT methodologies is to hold a privileged focus on secondary problems, often emotional in nature (Hayes & Hofmann, 2018). A feature of standard CBT is instead to focus part of intervention on internal factors of the primary problem (i.e. bias and schemas) (Beck, 1975; Dobson, 2010). When considering CBT for anxiety disorders, for instance, a nuanced difference between a standard and a contemporary approach may be as follows.

Standard approach

- Psychoeducation on anxiety
- Monitoring anxious responses in a given context
- Internal-external exposure to feared stimuli
- Identification and challenge of thoughts, assumptions, and their consequences
- Identification and challenges of schemas

Contemporary-advanced approach

- Identification of thoughts, whilst observing and distancing self from them
- Develop awareness in the present moment
- Develop an awareness with a focus towards own valued direction
- Differentiate between appraisals specific to a situation and personal values
- Advance our ability to differentiate between internal and external control
- Develop the ability to differentiate between primary and secondary problems and related interventions

4.5 Trends on Integrative Interventions

An increasing number of psychotherapists feel the requirement for the development of integrative psychotherapy (Hayes et al., 2020). A well-defined psychotherapy integration model represents the Holy Grail for a psychotherapist, as it was in the mind of APA division twelve when they defined evidence-based treatments (Sturmey & Hersen, 2012). Integrative psychotherapy focuses on incorporating several features and constructs that emerge and that are not well integrated and contradicting each other, currently.

Psychological disorders may be considered as "single" entities and pathologies, considering the significant comorbidity that each patient presents with during assessment. This leads clinical psychologists to consider broad perspectives, thus considering clinical clusters or the notion of spectrum, although the latter is not univocally represented amongst authors and researchers (Hayes et al., 2020).

Within this perspective, the aspects of the Big Five Model may be sufficiently universal and shareable with desirable convergence of theoretical contributions, to advance each Trait and repercussions on several psychological aspects (Barlow, Sauer-Zavala, Carl, Bullis, & Ellard, 2014).

The notion of Flexibility vs. Rigidity lends itself well as an operational criterion to differentiate between normality and dysfunction.

Traits may be rigid and result in dysfunctions in adjustments and achievement of personal goals (Barlow et al., 2014). Traits are determined by behaviours and coping strategies that individuals utilise in facing challenges and frustration posed by key meaningful aspects and that always concern Self-Worth.

Aspects of Self-Functioning and Interpersonal Relationships, as also included in DSM-5 (American Psychiatric Association [APA], 2012), are variables of mental states and previous coping strategies, which influence ways of interpreting contexts, choices, and individual relationships. Those aspects of the Self-Functioning and Interpersonal Relationships hold the role of epiphenomenon and capture a snapshot of the dynamic between schemas and consequences of coping strategies.

From this perspective, notions such as cognitive schemas, life themes, negative themes, "stories," and idiosyncratic ideas are Procrustean in nature, thus enforcing uniformity or conformity without regard to natural variation or individuality.

Furthermore, often schemas express general rules or vague judgments, and schema content and expression of Traits are mistaken with coping strategies (Hayes & Hofmann, 2018). This is often observed in research, by utilising questionnaires and tools to measure and quantify Traits, schemas, strategies, evaluations, and behaviours (Smith et al., 2004).

Rarely patients' difficulties can be conceptualised within a particular disorder (depression, panic, social anxiety, OCD, ill health anxiety, etc.) (Barlow et al., 2014). Clinicians evidenced that aspects of a given formulation are integrated into other formulations as part of a complex clinical picture, from which it emerges (or it should emerge) the clinician's perspective in comprehending the patient's perspective, thus formulating why he suffers in a certain way.

All of this incentives a clinician to seek an integrative perspective of technical and theoretical aspects useful and effective, so they may better meet overall psychotherapeutic clinical needs. On one hand, these aspects are applied to approaches and techniques, even with a different terminology; on the other hand, there are subjective methods to place and propose a change in perspective.

4.6 Narrative Themes in Psychotherapy

Therapists might build their own set of metaphors and modus operandi to encourage and foster change in perspectives. We shall briefly explore these ideas.

When reading different authors, we note that they have developed their own toolkit of stories and narratives. Some metaphors utilised are adapted from well-known stories or myths. Others are instead purposely created by clinicians with the intent to direct interventions within specific aspects of the problem: a belief, conflict, a paradox, and so forth.

One of the stories we utilise is concerned with the relativity of perspectives and opinions; this is the story of the nurse and the patient who suffers from dementia. An elderly gentleman suffers from severe dementia and is admitted to a nursing home. He is looked after by a nurse who is dedicated to do her best. The gentleman addresses the nurse in an offensive way; however, the nurse comports herself with compassion and professionalism and focuses on assisting the patient. What do we learn from the nurse? What is her perspective? How can we learn from her perspective and adapt it when dealing with criticism? This is a story that is easy to understand and has the advantage of promptly addressing the core problem.

Another story is the metaphor of the screwdriver. The premise is that there are practical problems that have practical solutions and psychological problems that have psychological solutions. When tightening a screw, we look for a screwdriver and try. If the screwdriver is not the correct size, we try another one or we adapt the one we have. Nothing else is required to tighten a screw. The learning point is that when we face actual problems, albeit significant and frustrating, we may have to seek practical solutions, rather than psychological ones.

A well-known story, although adapted, is the story of the fish and the hook. There are two fishes, one is young and naïve and the other is older and wise. They see the bait, but not the hook. The young one is inclined to eat the bait and is trapped by the hook. The older fish knows that this is a hook and therefore a painful trap. He therefore decides to continue as nothing had happened and focus on what is important to him. The learning point is that we have the ability to identify negative thoughts and traps, i.e. hooks, by adopting a perspective based on distancing ourselves from our mental states, without affecting our efforts to continue to work towards what is important to us.

A useful story is the story of a bunch of flowers. A woman, Lucy, would like to be gifted flowers from her partner, but she never receives them. One day Lucy loses her temper and reminds her partner that she would like to receive flowers. He asks Lucy why she never asked him before, given that she desired them so much. Lucy reprimands him stating that she had to remind him and therefore this is no longer a spontaneous gift. The learning point is that if we wish to receive something spontaneously, it is better not to be prescriptive, but to subtly communicate that we wish to receive a gift. Clearly it is not always possible to obtain what we wish for, but we may contribute to increasing the likelihood of obtaining something if we do what is within our power and compromise.

A very useful story is "back from the future." The story suggests imagining that whilst dealing with a challenging situation, a person decides that he will meet himself in the future, 10 years later. The person may want to seek advice from his future self. However, his future self might reassure him by telling him that everything will be solved and that after a prolonged period of time he will be able to clearly see what is happening currently.

We often ask our patients, "What do you think your future self will tell you?" Human beings concur that everything is going to be solved and will be able to evaluate things clearly. In this case, the message is clear; we tend to catastrophise in the spur of the moment, thus switching to emergency mode, whilst with time we have the opportunity to experience a clearer and broader perspective.

Several stories are created at the moment, depending on therapists' intentions and the nature of the psychological intervention. Several stories are adapted from other authors' metaphors (Hayes, Strosahal, & Wilson, 2012) and so forth, until they merge with oral narratives and traditions.

4.7 Mental States

How can we integrate primary and secondary psychological problems with ABC? It is essential to consider both from a formulation and psychological intervention perspective that our patients and clients focus and therefore mental state may change.

Identification of secondary psychological problems is extremely important both for the formulation of clinical cases and for psychological therapy planning. We may categorise secondary psychological processes depending as to whether they are focused on emotional states or mental states, or evaluation of self or coping strategies.

On careful observation, a secondary problem may lead to other ramifications. For instance, when a patient or a client is worried that he may become unwell, as he thinks he will lose control of self, the resulting anxiety (problem secondary to emotional state) will be associated with perceptual attentional processes and intrusive cognitions (problem secondary to cognitive processes), which will be associated to safety-seeking behaviours and avoidance strategies (problem secondary to coping and its consequences).

These four secondary problems or maybe three, if we associate emotional states to cognitive processes, are distinct aspects only from an instrumental and pragmatic perspective, as differentiating between them facilitates planning of specific interventions.

Our reaction to our responses is in reality a whole response that may be more or less relevant from time to time or in each individual. We might determine that a problem is present when we notice changes in our mental state. This is also true in general for the kind of interpretation and the meaning attributed by individuals, what he tries to do and what is his goal. Let's focus on generic categories of meaning:

- Loss
- Threat
- Injustice

In relation to a certain goal, the identification of loss related to a certain context, i.e. a bereavement, loss of personal effectiveness, of power, or role, or a drift in a relationship, is evaluated as realistic, and therefore as something that is happening or has already occurred. This activates the individual's resources and his ability to evaluate advantages or disadvantages of the situation.

What might be subsequently determined is the result of an estimation of a person's ability to control the situation, i.e. if there is something I can do, I will do it. Otherwise, I should accept this event and I can interpret it as an event that is out of my control and power and that is irrespective of me as a person.

A person may therefore accept the loss and its resulting psychological responses, reactions, and functioning associated with the behaviour inherent to that given cognitive and emotional state. A person may not, however, accept the loss, and its resulting psychological reactions and responses inherent to the psychological aspects of such loss. At this point, a person may give himself a goal not to lose, or to pursue the loss, or to distract himself from loss and oppose normal responses caused by suffering. In this phase, we note secondary problems both related to

- Emotional and cognitive states (intrusive thoughts, fantasies, and memories)
- Evaluative and schema aspects of the self
- Dysfunctional coping strategies

Danger and Threat, Fault and Injustice follow similar patterns.

Would it be possible to refer to this differentiation as a Standard Model as it presents with features common to several problems? Each person may have problems that have a focus on a specific primary problem. A person might interpret an emotional reaction as a problem, or thinking about something, or behaving in a certain way in a certain context. All these aspects may be considered problematic and trigger secondary psychological problems. Analysis of secondary problems is different from psychopathology based on categories. For instance, a person suffering from panic may be critical towards himself for being "too scared" (secondary problem), or a person suffering from depression may criticise himself for being "too depressed" (secondary problem).

A secondary problem concerning hypervigilance as a cognitive process may be present in most mental disorders (Johnson-Laird, Mancini, & Gangemi, 2006). Specific content of secondary problems is probably a characterising feature of macro-psychopathological areas, such as anxiety, depression, and psychosis, more so than within clinical conditions within the same macro-area. Panic and social anxiety might have more similar secondary problems than an anxiety disorder and a psychotic disorder, which are less similar but not entirely different.

Effective interventions for secondary problems depend on several factors. In the first instance, secondary problems are psychological problems, as primary problems: this means that they can be formulated as ABC. In CBT, a primary ABC and a secondary ABC are not qualitatively different (Dell'Erba & Nuzzo, 2010; Dobson, 2010). Whenever within a secondary problem one of its features is perceived and evaluated as a threat, the primary problem remains in the background, whereby attentional and cognitive biases remain focused on the secondary problem. Furthermore, to act on a secondary problem, it is important to consider that human beings have a focus and an object, a psychological problem and a part of it.

This vague consideration is a psychoeducational intervention, which prepares the therapeutic ground for other interventions. It is necessary to create distance with respect to the primary problem as Beck observed at the beginning of the 70s (Dobson, 2010).

A person experiencing a latent secondary problem tends to fluctuate between the object of the primary and secondary problem. In CBT, it has only recently been placed at the core of psychological analysis and formulation. The context where the need to consider fluctuating mental states in conflict or partially separated is the understanding of personality disorders, although this kind of formulation is not clearly specific to personality disorders, but to problems experienced by humankind.

4.8 Personality Disorders in Psychotherapy

Personality disorders are an open field in psychotherapy, as it is also observed in DSM 5 (APA 2012). Not only the concept of Trait or Personality Disorder is equivocal and lends itself to several perspectives, but also treatments and interventions may be less clear in comparison with other clinical problems such as anxiety, depression, eating disorders, and addictions (Hayes and Hofmann, 2020). However, both literature and clinical practice show that treatments and interventions are more homogenous and convergent, than the concepts and theoretical formulation themselves.

We shall attempt to summarise some aspects of clinical practice. A rough protocol might incorporate the following psychological aspects:

1 A focus on problems referred by patients should be reformulated as psychological problems. Often patients describe practical problems that require practical solutions and expertise, but not a clinical psychologist. Psychological problems may be categorised as primary and secondary ABCs, so that meaning, evaluation, and cognitive processes may emerge at different levels and in several respects

2 Metacognitive functioning and self-reflective aspects of our own mind and the others'. The ability to think about our own mind and the others' is a benefit to human beings in terms of better global functioning and quality of life (Boniwell, 2012). Conversely, challenges encountered in comprehending our own mind and the others', along with the components of the functioning of our own mind and the others', decrease opportunities to comprehend and to act, thus decreasing our ability to be effective and to control our valued sense of direction. In fact it is correlated with increased psychological suffering. The internal features of metacognitive functioning are linked to the ability to differentiate between

- A model A-C and a model B-C
- Hypotheses and evaluations
- What is within our control and what is not
- Our perspective and other person's perspective

To conclude, metacognitive functioning in the context of effective treatment for personality disorders consists in understanding our own mind and the others' (Carcione et al., 2016; Lemma et al., 2011; Safran & Muran, 2000; Young et al., 2003).

3 Therapeutic relationship. It is also essential to capture indicators and cues of threats to therapeutic relationship. This might allow the therapist to focus on these indicators and on relational exchanges in session, so they may be explored in relation to the patient's difficulties. The

rationale for focusing on the therapeutic relationship is to maintain the relationship by preventing or repairing eventual ruptures. According to Safran and Muran (2000), feelings or challenging behaviours, with underlying hostility and manipulation or avoidance strategies, might have a connotation of rejection and discouragement

The therapist's ability to be thoughtful and able to identify those signals and place them at the core of therapeutic exchanges to repair the relationship is considered essential in the literature regarding this kind of disorders (Carcione et al., 2016).

There are three features regarding this aspect that can be summarised as follows:

* Identify confrontation – challenges or avoidance
* Relationship to own personal theme through patterns
* Focus on personal themes

Identification of personal themes is crucial (Young et al., 2003). Personal themes are concerned with a patient's cognitive schemas, his coping strategies that appear dysfunctional, but make sense from a patient perspective and therefore may be validated, and link with the patient's life story.

Personal themes may be unique or characterised by several aspects. It is crucial to identify an aspect that is linked to the seminal dysfunctional pattern. There are several ways to capture personal themes, through questionnaires, for instance (Smith et al., 2004). However, the main one is clinical assessment and conceptualisation of critical incidents. Personal themes validated by therapists constitute the main ground for action or intervention of distancing and defusion of inflexible perspectives that paralyse the patient.

A further intervention might be the utilisation of a tool that can support timely comprehension from a patient's perspective, such as ABC or Polk's ACT Matrix (Polk & Schoendorff, 2014) or other models that facilitate the understanding of a collaborative work. Polk's Matrix and its variants are particularly effective in this regard (Polk & Schoendorff, 2014).

It is important that all is redirected towards general aspects to focus on the following:

* Understanding of the self and the others
* Note and accept interior experiences and external factors
* Focus efforts towards a valued sense of direction for the patient

Lastly, in personality disorders there is a specificity between different disorders, even if this is not particularly marked.

What emerges is the presence of significant superimposed aspects in the several personality prototypes and the emergence of general clusters such as impulsivity, manipulation, insecurity, dependency, detachment, and excessive emotivity. A way of synthesising this can be considering the following three aspects:

- Self-acceptance
- Ability to self-control
- Kindness – amiability

These are common features of all human beings, but it is rare that they are present in a single individual.

When working with personality disorders, there is an expectation that aspects of life stability should be identified; this is not the case when working with clinical disorders. This theoretical model (i.e. to differentiate between Traits and disorders or personality disorders and clinical disorders) is dubious and unsatisfactory (Hayes et al., 2020).

We may also utilise the construct of Traits or Level of Functioning of the Self (DSM5, APA, 2012) or the construct of Personality Disorder. However, it is unclear as to what differentiates a personality disorder from a clinical disorder, such as depression, anxiety, or addiction. We invoke co-morbidity to exit such bottlenecks, and associated conditions, although we are aware that this does not clarify this theoretical difference. When we identify Traits, they need to be specific; however, this is not what happens when assessing and diagnosing patients.

It seems that certain vague and blurred features are variably present in all patients. What we can do is to determine with certainty who does not present with certain features. The outcome is the identification of individuals who face several challenges, whilst tolerating their own emotional reactions, and the inevitable small idiosyncrasies and dips in their lives.

We do not believe that existing symptoms are crucial, required constructs to psychopathology. They might capture the surface of personal themes, mere lifestyle characteristics, determined by our own personal stories. It is likely that inflexible coping strategies and long-standing challenges in understanding self and others may be useful elements. A further indicator may be represented by the focus "not to feel X," for clinical disorders, and "not to be Y," for personality disorders. A distinct feature might be related to experiential avoidance versus avoidance of negative schemes, a tragic, unsustainable sense of self.

4.9 Case Example

Julie, a 26-year-old woman, with a Diploma of Higher Education in Health Care, and a patient in a Residential Psychiatric Assistance Community, was looked after by a Community Mental Health Team for pharmacological and psychotherapeutic treatment.

Julie's presentation was characterised by long-standing eating disorder, self-harming behaviours, and drug and alcohol misuse. Julie had been a victim of abuse within a relationship. Julie was followed up for psychological treatment by one of the authors (GLD), who formulated Julie's difficulties as borderline personality disorder.

Julie's presentation deteriorated in subsequent months, as she presented with marked emotional dysregulation, characterised by increase in anxiety and hopelessness.

Such crises were discussed in session to formulate meaning associated with behavioural patterns. With the progress of the psychological work, Julie was able to identify that she felt feelings of affection for the therapist and displayed sexualised behaviours towards him.

Therapy input identified that such behaviours were linked to Julie difficulties in experiencing a relationship emotionally not just sexually.

Emotional relationships with her father or a friend were forbidden or unthinkable from Julie's perspective. Julie subsequently disclosed that she and other family members suffered early and chronic abuse at the hands of her father. Furthermore, Julie's mother had displayed sexually extravagant and promiscuous behaviour. Julie disclosed that some sexual contact occurred between her and her father when she was 6 or 7 years old.

Further sessions were characterised by Julie's abrupt change of mental states from despair to anger; utilisation of trauma-based rewind techniques in the sessions contributed to the improvement of Julie's critical distancing from the perspective of "little girl Julie" to the present perspective of Julie as an adult woman session. Psychotherapy improved Julie's insight into early maladaptive schemas and unmet emotional needs as a young girl. Incorporation of attention training techniques, based on Mindfulness and ACT, resulted in further improvement in Julie's ability to identify and process past intrusive memories, rupture of family relationships, and her father's abusive behaviour. Julie's condition progressively improved, resulting in resigning from her position and venturing on a new job.

References

American Psychiatric Association. (2012). *Diagnostic and statistical manual of mental disorders (DSM 5)* (5th ed.). Washington, DC: APA.

Barlow, D.H., Sauer-Zavala, S., Carl, J.R., Bullis, J.R., & Ellard, K.K. (2014). The nature, diagnosis, and treatment of neuroticism: Back to the future. *Clinical Psychological Science, 2*(3), 344–365.

Beck, A.T. (1975). *Cognitive therapy and the emotional disorders.* Madison, CT: International Universities Press.

Beck, J.S. (2011). *Cognitive therapy: Basics and beyond* (2nd ed.). New York, NY: Guilford Press.

Boniwell, I. (2012). *Positive psychology in a nutshell: The science of happiness* (3rd ed.). London: McGraw-Hill.

Bordin, E.S. (1979). The generalizability of the psychoanalytic concept of the working alliance. *Psychotherapy: Theory, Research & Practice, 16*(3), 252–260.

Carcione, A., Niccolò, G., & Semerari, A. (2016). *Curare i casi complessi.* Bari-Roma: Laterza.

Castelfranchi, C., Mancini, F., & Miceli, M. (2002). *Fondamenti di cognitivismo clinico.* Torino: Bollati Boringheri.

Dell'Erba, G.L. (1998). *La Psicologia del Pensiero nelle Scienze Cognitive.* Rassegna Studi e Ricerche. Lecce: Istituto di Psicologia Università di Lecce.

Dell'Erba, G.L., Carati, M.A., Greco, S., Muya, M., Nuzzo, E., Gasparre, A. Amato, R. (2009). Le convinzioni di dannosità dell'ansia (CDA). *PsicoPuglia*, Ordine Psicologi Puglia, 3.

Dell'Erba, G.L., & Nuzzo, E. (2010). *Psicologia pratica.* Lecce: Pensa Editore.

Dobson, K. (2010). *Handbook of cognitive behavior therapy.* New York, NY: Guilford Press.

Ellis, A. (1994) *Reason and emotion in psychotherapy* (2nd ed.). New York, NY: Lyle Stuart.

Hadot, P. (2000). (contributor) *Manuale di Epitteto.* Torino: Einaudi.

Hayes, S.C., & Hofmann, S.G. (2018). *Process based CBT.* Oakland, CA: Content Press/New Harbinger.

Hayes, S.C., & Hofmann, S.G. (Eds.). (2020). *Beyond the DSM: Toward a process-based alternative for diagnosis and mental health treatment.* Oakland, CA: Context Press/New Harbinger.

Hayes, S.C., Hofmann, S.G., & Ciarocchi, J. (2020). A process-based approach to psychological diagnosis and treatment: The conceptual and treatment utility of an extended evolutionary meta model. *Clinical Psychology Review, 82*, 101908.

Hayes, S.C., Strosahal, K.D., & Wilson, K.G. (2012). *Acceptance and commitment therapy.* New York, NY: Guilford Press.

Johnson-Laird, P.N., Mancini, F., & Gangemi, A. (2006). A hyper-emotion theory of psychological illness. *Psychological Review, 113*(4), 822–841.

Legrenzi, P. (2019). *Storia della psicologia* (6th ed.). Bologna: Il Mulino.

Lemma, A., Target, M., & Fonagy, P. (2011). *Brief dynamic interpersonal therapy: A clinician's guide.* Oxford: Oxford University Press.

Mancini, F., & Giacomantonio, M. (2018). I conflitti intrapsichici. *Quaderni di Psicoterapia Cognitiva, 42*, 41–64.

Miceli, M., & Castelfranchi, C. (2014). *Expectancy and emotion.* Oxford: Oxford University Press.

Norcross, J. (2012). *Psychotherapy relationship that work* (2nd ed.). New York, NY: American Psychological Association.

Polk, K.L., & Schoendorff, B. (Eds.). (2014). *The ACT matrix: A new approach to building psychological flexibility across settings and populations.* Oakland, CA: Context Press/New Harbinger.

Robertson, D. (2019). *The philosophy of cognitive-behavioural therapy (CBT).* London: Routledge.

Safran, J.D., & Muran, J.C. (2000). Resolving therapeutic alliance ruptures: Diversity and integration. *Journal of Clinical Psychology, 56*(2), 233–243.

Sartre, J.P. (2003). *Being and nothingness* (H.E. Barnes, Trans.; 2nd ed.). London: Routledge.

Seligman, M.E.P. (1991). *Learned optimism*. New York, NY: Knopf.

Smith, E., Bem, D.J., & Nolen-Hoeksema, S. (2004). *Fundamentals of psychology*. Belmont: Wadsworth Publishing Co Inc.

Sturmey, P., & Hersen, M. (2012). *Handbook of evidence based practice in clinical psychology*. Hoboken, NJ: Wiley.

Wegner, D.M. (1989). *White bears and other unwanted thoughts: Suppression, obsession, and the psychology of mental control*. London: Penguin Press.

Weiss, J. (1990). The nature of the patient's problems and how in psychoanalysis the individual works to solve them. *Psychoanalytic Psychology*, 7(1), 105–113.

Wells, A. (1997). *Cognitive therapy of anxiety disorders: A practice manual and conceptual guide*. Chichester: Wiley.

Wells, A. (2008). *Metacognitive therapy for anxiety and depression*. New York, NY: Guilford Press

Young, J., Klosko, J.S., & Weishaar, M.E. (2003). *Schema therapy. A practitioner's guide*. New York, NY: Guilford Press.

Chapter 5

Psychotherapeutic Competencies in Integrative Psychotherapy

5.1 Training

How can we encourage our therapists in training to develop better and further competencies in understanding patients' and client's difficulties? This is a complex and multifaceted issue, concerning didactic pedagogical and supervisory aspects in psychotherapy. There are several competencies that might be created, enhanced, and evaluated. Some of them are generic to this profession, and others are more specific to the theoretical and clinical approach pertinent to Cognitive Behavioural Therapy (CBT) interventions. A possible solution may be to devise a series of competencies for further development and evaluation. Some are generic and concern the relational ability to develop and maintain relationship with others, the ability to practise within professional boundaries, as delineated by deontological practice and Codes of Conduct, and others are competencies that are acquired during training to be a psychologist: they concern fundamentals and foundation toolkits, i.e., assessment, psychopathology, cognitive processes, general and social psychology, evolutionary psychology, and neurosciences.

Other competencies are based on specific technical and theoretical CBT aspects, particularly the different approaches and orientations within CBT. These include process and modalities (why and how) on which interventions are built, i.e. cognitive restructuring, exposure, behavioural experiments, Socratic dialogue, psychoeducation, defusion, mindfulness, problem solving, and so forth (Hayes & Hofmann, 2018).

A further series of competencies is concerned with specific aspects such as disorder-specific protocols and procedures. In this context, knowledge and mastering of clinical procedures aimed at targeting specific conditions such as obsessive compulsive disorder (OCD), depression, and so forth.

To conclude, there are competencies required to be able to function and practise as therapists, such as focus on improving ourselves, learn to self-evaluate, ongoing improvement, and professional development, to adapt to complex contexts that are part of our profession.

DOI: 10.4324/9781003299226-6

Within the training environments context, there are competencies, aimed at building flexibility and integrating several effective aspects of psychotherapy. A cross competence is to be flexible and functioning and functioning as human beings, in such a way that normal everyday problems do not affect and interfere with professional boundaries. All these aspects should be nurtured, developed, encouraged, assessed, and evaluated (Roth & Pilling, 2008).

To understand patients' problems is the result of a series of general and specific competencies. In fact, a clinical case formulation is the result of a framework of intrinsic, built-in competencies, that might or might not be adequate to assess therapists' proficiency. Features of clinical case formulation are linked to the clinical and theoretical psychotherapeutic orientation.

What can be said about CBT. A few basics can cover a vast therapeutic field. These basics may be implicitly complex but may be considered as coordinates for case formulation.

- General and specific clinical information
- Problem description
- Conceptualisation of psychological factors
- Perpetuating factors
- History, including triggers and initial problem development
- Vulnerability and protective factors
- Treatment aims and goals
- Rationale, strategies, and therapeutic interventions
- Outcomes
- Therapeutic challenges
- Therapeutic relationship

These clinical formulation coordinates may be useful during psychotherapeutic training and supervision between experienced colleagues.

In several clinical contexts, supervision has specific competencies and is equipped with tools for evaluation of competencies. There are authors that have published on the effectiveness and monitoring of supervision, and these tools have been widely utilised over time (Borders & Brown, 2005; Falender et al., 2004; Milne & Dunkerley, 2010; Roth & Pilling, 2008).

An example is CTS-R Young and Beck (1980). A case example can be described as follows:

- Information gathering, including problems and diagnosis
- Patient history, including psychopathological anamnesis, family, and medical history
- Case formulation
- Precipitating factors

- Cognitive and behavioural factors that contribute to maintenance of the problem.
- History and development of cognitions and behaviours
- Assessment of strengths and vulnerabilities
- Working case formulation
- Treatment plan
- Intervention
- Therapeutic relationship
- Outcomes and Measures
- Comments

5.2 Personal Development

Once the necessary generic and specific competencies to practise psychotherapy are established, the following step might be to reflect on personal and professional boundaries between therapists and their trainees.

Personal psychotherapeutic training might be compulsory or not, depending on psychotherapy models' theoretical orientations. This is highly debated at international level (Roth & Pilling, 2008). Individual training may be required in addition to formal training delivered by Universities linked to Accredited Bodies. Formal competencies may be assessed according to certain criteria, which in turn may be translated to in knowledge and evaluated throughout delivery of clinical interventions, in keeping with competencies criteria and evaluations.

Although specific assessment competencies may be applied to evaluation criteria, and those competencies can be evaluated and translated into knowledge evaluated by formal examinations, variables concerning personal psychotherapeutic training are less defined. Furthermore, although general and specific psychotherapeutic competencies may be considered as knowledge that can be more or less assessed or evaluated, the variables or part of them are confined to health conditions of trainees, and may not be subject to evaluation that may result in exclusion or inclusion for accreditation purposes, for the reason that it may be considered discriminatory on health grounds (i.e. UK – The Health and Care Professions Council – HCPC, Code of Conduct). This may be often addressed with advice or with tacit agreement of the trainee but cannot be mandatory. However, adherence to HCPC and Code of Conduct is a fundamental prerequisite for Clinical Psychology students in the UK. Further mandatory requirements for students, to receive a Doctorate in Clinical Psychology award in the UK, are indicated as follows:

- Achieve satisfactory pass in their exams
- Pass placement: clinical placements performance is evaluated by supervisors
- Complete research projects and discuss their thesis, as part of a Viva

Resolutions are directed to protocols and supervision contracts between trainees and specific Clinical Doctorates.

A trainee might experience psychological problems but may be well qualified and able from a therapeutic perspective. For instance, a colleague may be sensitive to problems related to end of life, or eating disorders, but equipped as a therapist in other specialties. This is a frequent occurrence and may increase the likelihood of obtaining academic and professional qualification, provided that the trainee therapist is aware of his own boundaries and has a strong focus on self-improvement. This is different if a trainee suffers from psychosis, or a serious mental illness. In this instance, it is recommended that the trainee should defer the course, take care of his own health. Thereafter determine his condition and whether it may affect him in the educational setting. In this scenario, the award of qualification may be conditional, as training is usually deferred until there is a hurdle in the ability to stay in the educational setting.

5.3 Psychological and Psychotherapeutic Competencies

So far, we have focused on the importance of therapists' training and supervision based on specific and generic CBT competencies. What can be said about patients' psychological competencies?

Patients' psychological competencies, of individuals out with the psychology profession, are of the utmost importance. In this circumstance, we are referring to requirements pertinent to mental health. As mentioned earlier on, we are referring to the following considerations.

Personal values – sense of self-worth, and realistic evaluation of internal control. However, we may conceptualise general features that may aid identification as to whether a person can adapt to different life contexts and challenges, without being stuck in suffering, but live as meaningfully as possible. Further psychological factors are outlined be as follows:

- Discern the difference between perception of an external stimulus and its internal representation and meaning, including mental state; for instance, see a pen and think about a pen
- Notice and discern the difference between an avoidant behaviour due to an internal mental stimulus and pursuit of goals, and intents that are truly meaningful to a person. For instance, avoid meeting new people due to being timid, and face shyness to appreciate and enrich relationships with others
- Notice the difference between ourselves as conscious observers, and one or more aspects of our mind, for instance, "I observe and note a thought or a memory, and the thought or memory in itself."

- Ability to discern the difference between accepting emotional suffering, and frustration, compared to catastrophising towards our own reaction and events occurred
- Ability to differentiate between a value as a human being and pursuing a meaningful direction, rather than evaluating our self-worth and sense of self against effectiveness of goals achieved, for instance not to diminish our sense of self-worth, in case of lack of achievement, and consider self a failure
- Ability to differentiate between awareness of mentalising with other individuals, rather than perceive others as stimuli, and not as sentient beings with their own mind, for instance, perceive a person as described by his behaviour and not by his choices.

These key details can provide us with information and an idea of how psychologically equipped an individual is. This may allow him to face challenges, including relationships challenges (Lemma et al., 2011).

A person that lacks experience in these aspects is likely to present with several problems and will tend to get trapped in situations that are not within his power, rather than choosing what is within his power. DSM-5 (2012) describes at a very general level psychological features typical of a psychologically healthy individual, i.e. hold beliefs and values functional to his own and others' well-being. We think this is a good definition.

It is important to gauge the context within which the problem is experienced. If we are referring to psychological context, we suffer due to situations that are the core of their behaviour. When we identify frustration as a hurdle to achieving individual goals and intentions, then suffering is contextualised within the person's evaluation the individual makes in keeping with the situation he is experiencing. When we refer to hurdles related to pursuit of goals, we refer to what kind of goals are under threat or compromised. Our hypothesis is that the more relevant the goals are, the more intense the suffering will be. We are referring to analysis of the reasons behind behaviours, as indicated by Heider, and other cognitive psychologists (Hewstone, 1991). Furthermore, a goal may be more important, as it holds the foundation for the pursuit of another goal, and so forth. Therefore, when evaluation concerns internal control, a person might suffer for the self-criticism that he inflicts upon himself, and for the goals concerning himself that are considered as compromised or threatened (Miceli & Castelfranchi, 2014).

Our suffering is concerning our hope to pursue what is important to us. It is important to consider the difference between frustration, which is a normal response concerning the pursuit of a goal, and psychological suffering, that is the meaning that frustration acquires in a life context. We might, however, consider the problem concerning the causes of suffering, and mental disorders.

What might be also essential is to consider the ties that the mind may have and how it accesses information. In this context, neurological or neurocognitive disorders might add relevant consideration to psychological formulation. We would consider the problem of hope and representation, rendition of personal resources and resilience that a person has, in most instances suffering is linked to desperation.

5.4 CBT as a Gold Standard in Clinical Guidelines

CBT is widely recognised as an effective psychotherapy and is present in the guidelines as first-line or second-line treatment, when medication is also considered (Holmes, Neighbour, Tarrier, Hinshelwood, & Bolsover, 2002; NHS, 2019). What are the key CBT features that make it the treatment of choice over other psychological interventions?

CBT regards learning theories as the core foundation of its principles; these theories are its key ingredients, along with specific psychotherapeutic features (Dobson, 2010).

In vivo experience implies the development of learning through classical conditioning. Such learning may subside or be replaced by further learning, linked to previous learning from experiences. This is of fundamental importance for our functioning and survival of species, complex organisms, and individuals. Without this opportunity, we would be unable to anticipate contingencies. Subsequently, contingencies related to recurring situations in which we act, along with the information learned, equip us with a toolkit that enables us to discern what is ok from what is not, and what works from what does not, i.e. learning through operant conditioning.

We operate in an environment that pre-determines in several ways what works in relation to a goal and what does not. This key process is crucial to change unhelpful and dysfunctional behaviours. However, it is crucial to understand what information and what drive (motivation, aims, intents and goals) maintain certain behaviours. There is a reason why we act or behave in a certain way, and why a person has learned that certain information is ok, in relation to a specific goal.

Lastly, when we have fertile, extensive foundations of information, we do not need to "reinvent the wheel," we may infer new strategies from previous information. This way of working, learning through conceptualisation, enriches our knowledge database and significantly speeds up information acquisition and goal achievement (Norcross & Goldfried, 2019).

We described basic learning principles, which are of fundamental importance in CBT, as through each one of these, we may intervene through psychotherapeutic interventions (Hayes et al., 2020). For instance, if I have been involved in a car crash in a certain place, I automatically memorise a sequence of features linked to the traumatic event, i.e. the place, how I felt, my perception of the moment, what I was doing, and what I had planned to do. All of this will be associated with trauma through conditioning.

If I will be able to bear this process in mind, with patience, and I can continue to function well and pursue my goals, this incident will be normalised, associations will subside and will be extinguished, and this will remain an unpleasant memory.

If I resist and oppose these processes, avoiding, for instance, certain places, or try to suppress certain thoughts, or intensely trying to oppose certain emotional states, I will build a trap, despite experiencing a temporary relief. This trap will prevent or will decrease my ability to function, causing secondary problems.

It is crucial to comprehend normal psychological functioning, and this is a crucial, super efficacious aspect of CBT. Most CBT interventions have as goal restoration of normal functioning and a steady, gradual decrease of safety behaviours, including avoidance, both directly, and through numerous ways that individuals have to inflexibly avoid daily aspects of their living experience (Carcione et al., 2016; Hofmann et al., 2012).

5.5 Case Example

Giorgio is a 41-year-old Civil Engineer, he is married to a colleague, and they have a three–year-old daughter. Giorgio is an only child; he did not present with a history of psychiatric disorders but presented with perfectionist personality traits of adaptive nature. Giorgio remained locked in a sauna when his wife and daughter were in their hotel room. Giorgio could not open the door, but eventually managed to break out: this resulted in a fractured arm.

Giorgio developed Panic attacks and Agoraphobia approximately 10 days after this incident. In the subsequent four months, Giorgio started to present with marked anxiety symptoms, characterised by avoidance of media news.

Giorgio sought GP and Psychiatry consultations; he did not report any benefit from the initial psychiatrist input and sought further psychiatric consultation.

Giorgio was referred to one of the Authors, GLD, by the second psychiatrist.

Psychological assessment indicated that Giorgio's clinical presentation was in keeping with Panic Disorder, Agoraphobia, Borderline Personality Disorder. Furthermore, Giorgio experienced mild Generalised Anxiety Disorder, with mild perfectionist traits.

Preliminary sessions focused on psychoeducation and understanding of triggers, caused by rumination regarding fear of experiencing Panic attacks and safety behaviours, particularly health seeking behaviours.

Subsequent sessions focused on in vivo exposure, along with cognitive restructuring of catastrophic misinterpretation regarding physical symptoms and normal anxiety. Further therapeutic focus was based on worry and avoidance of misfortune.

Giorgio developed an increased ability to understand how mental states change and fluctuated between different problems: such ability developed along with Giorgio's understanding of how worry became pervasive in his life.

Functional analysis of dysfunctional, anxiety driven, cognitive strategies, revealed Giorgio's profound concern and increased sense of responsibility in protecting his wife and daughter from any misfortune. Overinflated, increased sense of responsibility was threatened by accident, as Giorgio felt he was unable to protect his family. Understanding of these processes and role of avoidance, including not giving self-permission to be unwell, resulted in Giorgio being able to resume his normal life, further to treatment.

References

American Psychiatric Association. (2012). *DSM-5*. Washington DC: APA Publishing.

Borders, L.D., & Brown, L.L. (2005). *The new handbook of counselling supervision*. Mahwah, NJ: Lahaska/Lawrence Erlbaum.

Carcione, A., Niccolò, G., & Semerari, A. (2016). *Curare i casi complessi*. Bari-Roma: Laterza.

Dobson, K. (2010). *Handbook of cognitive behavior therapy*. New York, NY: Guilford Press.

Falender, C.A., Cornish, J.A.E., Goodyear, R., Hatcher, R., Kaslow, N.J., & Leventhal, G., … Grus, C. (2004). Defining competencies in psychology supervision: A consensus statement. *Journal of Clinical Psychology*, *60*, 771–785.

Hayes, S.C., & Hofmann, S.G. (2018). *Process based CBT*. Oakland, CA: Content Press/New Harbinger.

Hayes, S.C., Hofmann, S.G., & Ciarocchi, J. (2020). A process-based approach to psychological diagnosis and treatment: The conceptual and treatment utility of an extended evolutionary meta model. *Clinical Psychology Review*, *82*, 101908.

Hewstone, M. (1991). *Causal attribution: From cognitive processes to collective beliefs*. London: Wiley.

Hofmann, S.G., Asnaani, A., Vonk, I.J., Sawyer, A.T., & Fang, A. (2012). The efficacy of cognitive behavioral therapy: A review of meta-analyses. *Cognitive Therapy and Research*, *36*(5), 427–440. doi:10.1007/s10608-012-9476-1

Holmes, J., Neighbour, R., Tarrier, N., Hinshelwood, R.D., & Bolsover, N. (2002). All you need is cognitive behaviour therapy? Commentary: Benevolent scepticism is just what the doctor ordered commentary: Yes, cognitive behaviour therapy may well be all you need commentary: Symptoms or relationships. Commentary: The "evidence" is weaker than claimed. *BMJ*, *324*(7332), 288–294.

Lemma, A., Target, M., & Fonagy, P. (2011). *Brief dynamic interpersonal therapy: A clinician's guide*. Oxford: Oxford University Press.

Miceli, M., & Castelfranchi, C. (2014). *Expectancy & emotions*. Oxford: Oxford University press.

Milne, D., & Dunkerley, C. (2010). Towards evidence-based clinical supervision: The development and evaluation of four CBT guidelines. *The Cognitive Behaviour Therapist, 3*, 43–57.

NHS. (2019). *Overview - Cognitive behavioural therapy*. Retrieved from https://www.nhs.uk/mental-health/talking-therapies-medicine-treatments/talking-therapies-and-counselling/cognitive-behavioural-therapy-cbt/overview/

Norcross, J.C., & Goldfried, M.R. (2019). *Handbook of psychotherapy integration* (3rd ed.). New York, NY: Oxford University Press.

Roth, A.D., & Pilling, S. (2008). Using an evidence-based methodology to identify the competences required to deliver effective cognitive and behavioural therapy for depression and anxiety disorders. *Behavioural and Cognitive Psychotherapy, 36*(2), 129–147.

Young, J., & Beck, A.T. (1980). *Cognitive therapy scale. Rating manual*. Philadelphia, PA: University of Pennsylvania. Psychotherapy Research Unit.

Chapter 6

Hope, Resilience, and Acceptance in Integrative Psychotherapy

6.1 Hope

In what way is Hope relevant as a psychological construct?

Frustration and suffering depend on how we give meaning and evaluate the opportunity to achieve our goals. I may not suffer and be well if I consider opportunities and translate them into action. We are aware that living our life with the intent to achieve specific goals may be motivating and energising in the short term, but disappointing in the long term, whenever we have not achieved those goals. A person is likely to experience disappointment, dejection, and hopelessness, should he not achieve his goals. Conversely, we know that Hope of doing something in a direction towards our valued goals is one of the causal factors or human suffering, when there is negative evaluation attached.

There is an important reflection to consider, a goal may or may not be achieved, I may invest resources and time to achieve it and measure how long it takes me to achieve it. A specific goal may not be achieved, at which point I may substitute it with another goal. I note immediately that these are not the kind of goals that represent or capture a sense of direction in life and become the object of hopeful thoughts.

Hope is built on goals, and that might lead to hopelessness, should this intent be based on measuring our self-worth. They are not achieved in themselves but are substantiated by behaviours and responses; we often define them as Values (Dahl, Plumb, Stewart, & Lundgren, 2009). Although hopelessness is a major cause of human suffering, we may equally regard Hope as one of the most important factors in mental health (Boniwell, 2016).

Beck proposed that one of the key indicators and precipitating factors in suicide is hopelessness, despair that is. He also developed a questionnaire in this regard (Beck, Kovacs, & Weissman, 1979). We might therefore reflect that finding Hope is essential in maintaining life. Hope is what keeps us alive; it is associated with a good, full, and meaningful life. Hope also tells us that we are following our valued sense of direction. The problem is not

DOI: 10.4324/9781003299226-7

Hope in itself, but the Hope that our values and goals are achievable and are devised as such. Arguably, a person might think that based on a judgement or feedback, he is not "adequate" and will not be living a life according to his values and what matters to him the most.

In what respect is it possible that something might pose a threat towards a value or a meaningful sense of direction? As mentioned before, a goal may be achievable or not; a further goal may be devised should the outcome of the initial goal not be favourable, so we may continue to proceed towards what is of meaning to us. A value, on the other hand, is fulfilled in the moment we comprehend what is important and meaningful to us. A value cannot be compromised by an event, by an evaluation of performance, or critical feedback, the latter being always specific and not generalisable to other areas of life. Confusion between goals and values might lead to the collapse of our meaningful direction. Life might cease to be meaningful, resulting in reduced motivation within the most basic, yet essential, aspects of our lives. This is an existential crisis that morphs into despair when goals and values continue to be considered as a duty, an obligation, and conditional to our personal self-worth.

To conclude, the confusion between values and objectives may lead to loss of meaning and internal attribution of personal inability, or subjective perception of an insurmountable hurdle, may result in despair in our minds (Seligman, 2018).

The opposite occurs in meaningful life. Let us think about some scenarios to illustrate this point.

- A student sits an exam and believes to be poorly prepared. If he thinks that the exam outcome will be a failure, he will feel dejected. However, he might have hoped to sit the exam again at the next exam diet and remain motivated to follow his valued sense of direction. If we hypothesise that the student still thinks that he will fail and does not envisage a hopeful prospective future, but a despairing one instead, he will not be able to sit the exam; this might result in compromising his meaningful sense of direction, thus resulting in an eventual negative exam outcome as powerful threat. A negative, self-critical evaluation will be at the foundation of such hopelessness, along with a life void of meaning

    We focused at length on dysfunctional appraisal and secondary problems activated within individuals within these kinds of scenarios. It is worth considering that the Hope to re-sit the exam and envisage a meaningful life is empowering and provides comfort in other aspects of this student's life.
- When psychotherapists work with patients with severe neurodegenerative diseases, such as Alzheimer's, they hold on to Hope that their work is meaningful to their patients and caregivers, despite the fact that there will be a poor prognosis

Hope is a precious mindset. It is crucial to address it well and that it remains linked to what is within our power.

6.2 Values and Sense of Directions – Meaningful Lives

Hope is a component of meaningful life. What are the other components? A meaningful life remains as such when a person is focused on what really matters to him, making choices without feeling under pressure, under covert persuasion, and accepting to act with what is within his power.

Accepting frustration as a possibility that occurs out of our control results in being synchronised and focused on what matters to us. However, if we do not accept frustration and we appraise it as a value or a threat to our values, we feel that our life is no longer meaningful. Thus, a meaningful life does not mean searching for ephemeral pleasures, distractions, drugs or alcohol misuse, possess wealth, buy nice goods, and so many other opportunities akin to temporary gratification. A meaningful life is about being inspired and feeling empowered to be in the present. I feel that my life is meaningful, and I choose to be a person of a certain kind, with a direction that truly matters to me.

We might add, "focus on what is within your control, or accept frustration, a negative event that is not within your control." These notions seem Stoic in nature, and they are, but are also suggestions built on quintessential contemporary cognitive psychology themes (Robertson, 2019). Furthermore, there are circumstances where we might say "your responses are human," "accept frustrations and let go of the rest."

We note that there are two different layers in such assertions:

- The first is linked to the primary problem, i.e. the problem that we experience within a context, within the world, and therefore the ultimate cause of our frustration
- The second is addressed to secondary problems, i.e. problems concerning emotional reactions, mental states, our own self-evaluations, and recursive dysfunctional coping strategies.

Therefore, a meaningful life might be built of the following psychological competencies (Dell'Erba & Nuzzo, 2010):

- Awareness of our abilities and self-control
- Ability to distance ourselves from our mental states
- Stability within our core values
- Acceptance of external frustrations
- Humility and flexibility as modus operandi

This might be the psychological foundation of a meaningful full and serene life (Dell'Erba & Nuzzo, 2010).

There are other lenses that offer further detailed perspectives of meaningful life, as indicated by Seligman (2018) and professionals who contributed to the development of Positive Psychology and Prospective Psychology; these aspects are concerned with how to support people to live well and meaningfully. Being healthy without worries or illnesses does not necessarily mean live a purposeful life, a good life. When supporting patients or clients not to develop recursive problems and wisely accept realistic frustrations, we have not reflected or considered how we may spend our existence in a full and meaningful way.

As Seligman stated (2018, p. 294): "curing the negatives does not produce positives." Positive Psychology presents some aspects that merit to be understood and implemented. What are they and what is their relation to CBT? Selingman and his numerous collaborators identify some fundamental universal themes of strength in humankind. They are extremely frequent and are captured by the acronym PERMA:

Positive Emotion
Engagement
Relationships
Meaning
Achievements

These themes may be considered as aspects of life that contribute to and substantiate who we want to be and how we want to live. We should focus on these, investing on our strengths. This aspect of meaningful life and well-being is founded on psychological competencies explored earlier, and that matter when we differentiate between mental health disorders and recursive psychological suffering.

CBT is a set of well-developed and sophisticated psychological treatments, which are based on such psychological competencies and target several psychopathological disorders. Furthermore, CBT is in tune with prospective and Positive Psychology. Acceptance and distancing being two core examples, which along with other specific procedures and psychological competencies, are key ingredients in the treatment of mental disorders and promote a meaningful life, focused and orientated on what really matters to individuals (Seligman, 2018).

6.3 Philosophical Foundations of Psychotherapy

CBT is a theoretical technical model derived from Psychoanalysis and Behaviourism and philosophical intuitions foundations, such as Stoicism, Kant, Popper, despite theoretical differences between them (Legrenzi, 2019).

Ellis and Beck attempted to preserve core aspects of the main approaches at the time and enrich them with an additional element not present until then, i.e. pure unadulterated work on cognitions, a trademark contribution of CBT (Robertson, 2019).

Philosophical intuition and foundations of CBT are crucial. The Stoic Zeno is the father of Metacognition (Robertson, 2019). Epoché, i.e. a suspension in judgement and Prosochē, i.e. the attitude and practice of attention, are the prelude to ABC, and interventions on B, both with regard to distancing self and disputing. Chrysippus' (cited by Seneca and Epictetus) metaphor of the dog and cart narrates (Robertson, 2019):

When a dog is tied to a cart, if it wants to follow it is pulled and follows, making such spontaneous act coincide with necessity; however, if the dog does not want to follow, it will be compelled to do so in any case. Thus, it is with men too: even if they do not want to, they will be compelled in any case to follow what is destined.

In this thought experiment, if the dog wants to follow the cart he *must* follow the cart, even if he does not want to. This will be reprised by Ellis (1994), with regard to what is within and out with our control.

This is linked to the concept of distancing ourselves and to differentiate between the observing selves and the challenging the content of representation. Epictetus explicitly assigned a function of control of conscious representations and encouraged his disciple not to take for granted thoughts and meaning attributed to them (Hadot, 2000). This is an ABC that dates to around 100 BC.

It is useful to remind ourselves that each ACT concept developed by Stephen Hayes has Stoic support and references, which unfortunately are not acknowledged (Robertson, 2019).

A meaningful concept in Anglo Saxon CBT is already present in Epictetus and is at the foundation of his philosophy.

Within the Stoic Tripartition of Logic, Physics, and Ethics (Hadot, 2000; Robertson, 2019), Logic is founded on the metacognitive difference between the analysis of cognitive components, where the role played by intrusive thoughts is of particular significance.

Training of Stoic philosophers is anchored on the development of the ability to differentiate and identify their own thoughts and to maintain distance, whilst still pursuing direction based on defusion and values (ACT).

A further example is the Serenity Prayer according to Reinhold Niebuhr (Robertson, 2019).

God, grant me the serenity/courage to accept the things I cannot change, courage to change the things I can and wisdom to know the difference.

The first is based on ethics, Good is followed, which for the Stoics is the only possible Good (i.e. Morality, which is within his power, effort to achieve his Values).

The second is Physics; we are in its presence, follow its laws, and contemplate them (Acceptance).

The third is Logic; its intent is to possess content, in which we discern representations concerning what belongs to thought processes and what does not (Defusion, Self as an Observer).

Aristotle's legacy leads us to the current convergence between CBT and Positive and Prospective Psychology. Kant's work on Categories and Transcendental Aesthetic is the incipit of Cognitivism in general psychology (Legrenzi, 2019). CBT creatively adapts in its own way philosophical and intuitions and argumentations, often powerful and essential. We may refer to the role of Choice in Heiddegger and Sartre and subsequently in Hannah Arendt (Warburton, 2007).

Our choices and commitments, based on our power and control, provide existential momentum, direction and define action in relation to values. Values are thus operationalised.

These considerations may be extremely lengthy. However, it is worth considering that CBT has strong philosophical foundations and body.

What would be the outcome of Philosophy and CBT integration?

An example may be utilisation of ABC as a practicum.

When I perceive and identify a C, an emotion, I try to differentiate between A, a stimulus, from B, an assumption. Discerning between A and B results in me attributing a personal meaning, taking responsibility for my evaluation and subsequent choices.

Effect is powerful, immediate, and simple to understand and obtain. We may all practice to progressively develop this skill, as taught by Epictetus. We tend to shape the world with our own preconceived ideas, as we think it should be and therefore to expect what to find. This is normal, and it is best for us to function that way, we cannot always reinvent the wheel!

However, there is a difference between knowing this and bearing it in mind, and therefore always be aware of, that the balance between expectations and knowledge on the one hand and information and perception (discovery and experience) on the other hand, provides flexibility and ability to adapt to the contexts. A different matter is, however, not being aware and becoming enmeshed with our judgement and biases as if they were objective facts.

The ability to implement such discernment gives freedom of choice but also responsibility, freedom, and responsibility are coordinated with our autonomy as adults, as expressed by Kant (Warburton, 2007).

We are so used to taking for granted the way we relate to a context that we no longer pay attention to the fact that such modality is a subjective perspective.

A metaphor often used in this instance is to think about a fish who does not understand what water is, as it is its natural environment. Reality is what it is, regardless of our judgments.

Everything that follows frustration, that connotes a complaint, is our way to say NO, to oppose reality, to attempt to modify the external world.

However, each NO that belongs to what is within our control becomes a problem, an intent or a goal that can be achieved in practice and sustained by our commitment and doing our best.

When NO occurs in territory out of our control, then it anticipates disappointment and is void of rational thinking. An attempt to put this in practice from a psychological perspective is based on being aware of the B and the dichotomy between power and control.

After all, acting whilst remaining within what is in our power and control is an exercise in rationality and is suggestive of humility and modesty, awareness of our limitations, starting from looking from above and imagining what our perspective would be like if we looked at it with Zeus or Kosmos' eyes.

6.4 Frustration and Distress

The most salient aspects of an individual, his sense of self and value as a person, are generated from learning. Thoughts, feelings, and emotions are normal until we allow them to be, as we pursue our valued sense of direction. Or they might become abnormal to us, and we evaluate them as such.

Avoidance of our inner experiences brings an impoverishment, as we deprive and cut ourselves from life. By creating psychological traps that perpetuate themselves, blocking individual functioning and decreasing opportunities to experience contentment. This is a useful generic framework (Dell'Erba, Frascella, Leo, Mascellino, & Mariano, 2020).

In what way is it possible to focus on psychological problems without directly addressing mental health disorders? Would it be possible to isolate a pure psychological component, without an accompanying psychopathological one? Psychology is a core foundation of psychotherapy and applied psychotherapeutic interventions. It represents the foundation and in fact, understanding of mental states allows us to understand the mind, its functioning and relationships within people.

One of the basic aspects to start exploring psychological problems is Frustration. Frustration is the result of a loss, a failed expectation, or a goal not achieved. Frustration represents the non-coincidence between goal and acquisition, without considering thematic content such as danger, loss, and injustice. One of the most obvious reactions to frustration is to complain. Why do we complain? We all complain, every day, whilst taking for granted the foundation of this behaviour.

In what way complaints manifest themselves?

A phenomenology of complaints should include sharing, expressing or not expressing our own complaints. Sharing complaints takes place by giving an account of the frustrating event. Expressing the complaint consists in making visible and evident our disappointment, and giving ourselves permission, not always consciously, to become involved in the frustrating event.

To not express a complaint instead seems important to avoid a social judgement. All of this is in relation to the goal of complaint, i.e. what is the purpose and function of complaining, from the individual's perspective? What is the purpose of the complaint?

Complaining is a way of directly expressing pain and suffering. It might be meaningful to learn to discern between two different meanings and functions. To simply, directly, experience pain is the expected spontaneous reaction. We take this for granted, but we will focus on the following and its utilisation.

To protest and react as a consequence (meaning opposing to a consequence) to a desired but unachieved goal.

The reasons for complaining may be multifactorial, i.e., to protest, receive help, to become a victim and obtain advantages, to blame external circumstances, or be victims of misadventure. All these reasons may be powerful and deep-rooted so they can make a complaint and its modalities, a behaviour that is not explored and not reflected upon. Complaining also serves a social function to relocate ourselves within a group.

To what extent psychoeducation and social learning matters in processing frustrations and how much it affects complaints?

Psychoeducation in working with NO is obviously crucial. On the one hand, lack of acceptance or understanding regarding NO, and therefore, our own limitations is fundamental for our survival; on the other hand, full passivity and inaction might lead to not learning new information and taking initiative. Learning to process external NOs is a core learning experience. Hurdles are a part of normal life, not exceptional events, or occurrences that require bespoke solutions, there cannot be any other way around this. Within this perspective, normal life is conceptualised as an" up and down" in the valued direction of the individual.

However, there is a further perspective, hurdles are considered as injustice, and normal life is envisaged as void of them.

What does a perspective void of hurdles entail? In the first instance, it provides a false representation of our limitations and boundaries. Furthermore, lack of learning from NOs, and related hurdles throughout our lives, creates a focus on anticipating mishaps and setbacks in an excessively specialistic way, subsequently becoming increasingly hypersensitive. A path that leads to avoidance; in this instance, coping strategies will be focused on avoidance and to resist-oppose external "NOs," and personal boundaries and limitations.

What are the alternatives to this kind of resistance and avoidance? Our preferred alternative is the path to resilience.

6.5 Resilience

Resilience is both a condition and an attitude (Dell'Erba et al., 2020). Being resilient means to have a propensity to strengthen ourselves, whilst remaining orientated to our valued sense of direction. Or to consider a hurdle, a mishap, a setback as part of a path, without catastrophising or interpreting the NO, as a cue to our sense of self-worth. Resilience incorporates ups and downs, as part of ordinary life. The focus is to remain positioned on what matters to the person.

What does opt for a perspective based on resilience entail? Let us start by reflecting on the following.

Ongoing work on resilience is different from utilising and reinforcing resilience each time that a trauma or an accident occurs in the individual's life.

The most immediate kind of resilience is equivalent to coping strategies. There is a whole field of literature that is concerned with the features of well-being and ability to succeed as individuals (Dell'Erba et al., 2020).

A second kind of resilience is more specific and concerns what are the key factors that explain why some individuals recover sooner and at a faster pace from trauma, whilst other individuals are extremely upset and traumatised, or psychologically damaged.

A further consideration concerns asking ourselves if there are specific aspects where we show more resilience than others. Resilience is opposed to the concepts of adversity, negative events, trauma, and disaster. Whilst the notion of resilience is present nowadays to the extent that it has become a popular concept, its opposite, i.e. "inflexibility," although vague and generic, becomes hugely significant. In fact, there is always a context for resilience, and in particular, a context which also includes the negative event and the mind of the individual with its goals.

A fundamental difference at this point is that one part includes the fact that an event that is out of the power and control of an individual. The other part is where the event is connected to another goal, whether wanted or not, or part of an expectation.

In the first instance, a catastrophe and its negative evaluation are within the choices of preferences and goals of the individual, and not within the neutral action of Nature. From this perspective, it is hard to consider what is an unfortunate event, a catastrophe to us as individuals, it would be so also from an outlook from above. For example, is a virus unjust? Is an earthquake malevolent? A tsunami should not occur? Cancer is a woe? In all of these examples, it is crucial to establish what are the processes that play a role in these kinds of evaluation.

In Nature Good and Evil, Justice or Injustice does not exist. These are moral concepts that exist within psychological and social contexts, where there is an evaluation of Good and Evil.

The main point is to consider the individual, and thus all humankind, equipped with motivation, desire, duty, and awareness of their own condition. A negative event is considered as it threatens and prevents these goals, thus undermining individuals' lives and fulfilment.

A woe may be considered a frustration posed to the life plans of an individual, something that results in a setback, to the way to think about himself as a fulfilled individual, worthy to have lived.

Therefore, resilience has its own meaning, as it is an ongoing dynamic process of calibration and flexible reinvention of our life goals, the meaning of what is important to us and worthy of being pursued, so that our lives are worthy of being lived, despite its fragilities and vulnerabilities.

The aim of resilience is to maintain our life project alive, recalibrate it, and reposition it within the individual's valued direction (Dell'Erba et al., 2020). Furthermore, there is always something that may be learned from challenging circumstances, information that can be recuperated.

Psychologists defined this process as post-traumatic growth (Boniwell, 2016). This is a concept that has always been expressed in each culture for millennia. The growth and the message that can be learned from disadvantage is that what is important will still be there, it cannot be removed by anyone or by Nature.

It is important to spontaneously, not instrumentally capture such differences concerning the "dichotomy of control." For instance, a discovery occurs, it cannot be wanted or obtained, or forced. In fact, scientific discoveries occur throughout research projects that may last for years or not achieve the desired outcomes.

When an individual is resilient, he might tolerate the impact of the negative event (Boniwell, 2016). This person might also have the ability to wisely pace his involvement in action and pursuit of his goals; he is also content with what he has and is able to regulate the extent to which he decides to be content with what he can or cannot have.

To achieve contentment is to reach balance within a continuum of fault and excess. A resilient person is able to balance the excess of power and control with excess in the belief of not having choices in his life. Recalibrating this point means reframe the problem of control and power, within a balanced perspective, and reprise valued sense of direction. There are at least four ways of thinking that can promote quality of life and increase probability to remain oriented towards a meaningful life.

- To consider hurdles as opportunities to strengthen ourselves and utilise NOs as training opportunities of acceptance
- Premeditatio malorum. Premeditation of evils consists in imagining the worst-case scenario. This helps us to reframe and to reappraise the NO. This leads to developing gratitude, no matter towards whom or what and feeling at peace with ourselves

- Develop increased awareness of alternatives to strengthening tests and healthy psychological development. In this instance, it is important to capture the tunnel in which we might end up, without entering it fully. This point means to being able to identify the act of complaining, competition, focus on someone's incompetence, inflate facts as if we were writing a story
- Recognise our appraisals of primary problems, without activating secondary ones.

These considerations support each other; each one of them contributes to maintain our orientation towards what matters to us, even when mishaps, setbacks, NO, etc., become hurdles.

In what way can we envisage-devise interventions aimed to process traumatic events and ongoing social stressors? Interventions range from psychotherapeutic ones but also to perspectives, stances, and psychologically oriented frame of mind. In emergency scenarios, we all implement what is useful to individuals and populations. One of these strategies is to adopt and foster resilient perspectives. Dell'Erba et al. (2020) suggested that interventions might also include, talking, psychotherapy, messages on social media.

In the event of significant emergency or maladjustments, everyone is summoned, mobilised, to offer resources that are more useful to individuals and populations. One way of doing this is to adopt and encourage resilience in its different forms. We might consider different typologies of interventions, from social media to widespread communication several facets, which possess key messages geared to convey functional viewpoints (Dell'Erba et al., 2020).

- Tolerate frustration and increase tolerance by supporting individuals to renounce dubious claims and the expectation not to experience challenges experienced by all humankind
- Value our own resilience as a goal in itself
- Continue to do our best towards our valued sense of direction even in adverse circumstances and increased stress
- Consider that negative, stressful events are not within our power, but it is within our power to respond to such events. It is not useful to despair or fight against something that is outside our power, or control, but commitment and effort on useful actions and towards our valued sense of direction is within our control
- Persistence of negative events may have a cost, in terms of loss of social contacts, pleasurable activities, reduced ability to make autonomous choices, in the presence of negative limiting circumstances. This is also in the context of exposure to negative emotional states, such as boredom, frustration, anger, sadness, and fear associated with negative events.

Those costs may be validated and recognised as normal. Validation and normalisation, thus decreasing and discouraging subjective, negative evaluations, inadequacy, incumbent catastrophic events, etc.

- Personal costs of negative planetary events may be reframed within an altruistic perspective, and sense of community. Being part of a common effort to protect vulnerable individuals may promote and increase motivation, adding value (altruism), and personal meaning (it is worth it)
- Lack of control on other people's behaviours, in endemic challenging social situations. This can result in developing hostility, suspicious and aggressive behaviours towards others. It is important to identify such stances and hostile perspectives, reminding and encouraging ourselves to what is useful and meaningful to us and what is outside our power and control
- Another aspect is to consider that in emergency situations, not everything available is reliable. It is therefore essential to refer to official sources of information, and to accept and tolerate a degree of uncertainty on data provided; whilst it is important to obtain information, no information is perfect and definitive.
- In case of prolonged permanence at home or in a safe place, encourage social contact through phone, social media, and other means of communication. Human contact is essential to everyone and contributes to increasing a sense of control on our own lives, and on motivation towards what is important to all of us
- We do not all have the same resources or the same level of psychological resilience throughout emergencies or protracted restrictions. Everyone can make himself useful and support those who are vulnerable. Altruism and organising constructive social action can be a meaningful intervention
- Psychoeducation is also extremely important and constructive in the contact with others, through every means of communication. It is important to contrast and discourage everyone's including public figures, excessively polarised opinions, generalisation, and catastrophising, whilst encouraging adequacy and understanding of our psychological responses, recalibrating them towards a constructive and meaningful direction for everyone
- Identify and briefly clarify selective attention process, rumination, intrusive thoughts, and tendencies to act impulsively on the basis of rushed and biased evaluations. It is crucial to validate and normalise such psychological processes, in contexts pertinent to each individual
- Some individuals are at risk of stigmatisation and prejudice from certain parts of the population. Some social rules, professions, personal vulnerabilities like mental disorders or physical conditions, might limit access to assistance. These can all be perceived with fear towards

these individuals, thus developing excessive unjustified avoidance. It is important to validate the frustration, lack of gratitude and deprivation, which are encountered by these individuals

• Encourage a perspective to focus on life in the present moment give meaning to our days, as everyday's life, even in emergency situations,

All of these points seem to configure an Integrated Resilience Psychotherapy (Dell'Erba et al., 2020).

This is a CBT framework, but open to ideas and suggestions, which has shown to be rooted within understandable, effective, and advanced psychology. We would not overlook the philosophical aspect, rooted in Greek and Roman Stoicism like Seneca, Epictetus, Marcus Aurelius. who are the spiritual fathers of psychotherapy and of CBT. This opens opportunities to new practical solutions, for instance, developing psychological skills, to maintain resilience and flexibility. The general framework of general Clinical Psychology is to consider the big picture, a comprehensive view of individuals, not just mental disorders, or psychological aspects.

What practical points may be derived from Clinical Psychology and CBT, to contribute to Resilience and maintain orientation towards a meaningful life? Considering resilience means to discuss Prevention in Clinical Psychology, as it implies the understanding of what keeps us oriented towards a meaningful life, whatever the context or the presence of challenges.

The term resilience has been frequently used in recent years, both in psychology and in media. Etymology of resilience is from resalio, to get back on a horse if and when we fall, for instance. Resilience is a synonym of being sturdy, resistance, and as such is a term that is utilised in Medicine, Engineering, and other disciplines, indicating that an object or a system resumes its original form after a perturbing event. In psychology, resilience is the opposite of vulnerable and fragile and it alludes to both the ability to resist events and contexts that present disadvantages.

In summary, a resilient individual is someone who can adapt and thus position himself to the other end of the continuum of an individual that suffers from trauma, for instance.

This term can also be broadened by adding dealing with adversities whilst maintaining serenity and peacefulness. Psychological synonyms of resilience are perseverance, strength, energy, ability to adapt, flexibility, ability to tolerate distress, to recuperate, heal. Psychological opposites are vulnerability, weakness, and inability. From such terms we deduce that the concept of resilience can have several significant applications in psychology, although it requires robust formulation. Factors and features of resilience are

• Overcome problems such as neglect or financial challenges
• Live with daily stressful events

- Recuperate and heal from significant traumatic events
- Acquire meaning in life

Social support and access to meaningful personal relationships are important factors.

Protective factors may be external, such as social support, opportunity to express ideas, receive encouragement, validation, and Hope (Seligman, 2018). Individual factors are related to having a balanced view of self, of our abilities to accept and tolerate adversities, a good perception of ourselves as problem solvers, to have empathy, assertiveness, and the ability to communicate with others. Lastly, good self-regulation is associated with resilience. All these aspects are psychological competencies towards which an individual can improve and represent the foundation of a meaningful life.

6.6 Case Example

Sara is a 52-year-old woman; she is divorced and now in a same-sex relationship.

Sara does not have children; she has a degree in Politics and works as a Superintendent for the Italian Police. Sara's marriage ended due to her coming out as homosexual; divorce was amicable.

Sara's partner encouraged her to seek psychotherapeutic input and was seen by one of the authors (GLD), mainly due to frequent arguments with her colleagues and her working environment. Sara's presentation was in keeping with narcissistic personality disorder.

Beginning of therapeutic work was characterised by Sara's frequent challenges to her psychotherapist's role, whilst subtly undermining psychotherapy input.

Throughout sessions 7 and 8, Sara reflected that she experienced significant anger; she oversaw a case of fraud and reacted with anger to a colleague's criticism, by pushing his face. The situation was contained due to her colleague's response. Sara reflected that these episodes like these are increasingly frequent, and she is upset at her own reactions.

We explored Sara's meaning of her mental states, with an emerging theme of humiliation.

Suffering associated with feeling humiliated, linked to functional analysis of her personal story. Sara's story started with financial difficulties posed by the sudden death of both of her parents in rapid succession, when she was 18 years old, and studying for her final secondary school exams. Sara's parents were wealthy business owners. Sara's only brother went to the Netherlands, where he became a permanent resident and never returned to Italy. Sara's experience of financial difficulties, loss of status, considered herself demoted, along with the loss of her parents, significantly impacted on Sara. Sara compensated feelings of humiliation with a coping strategy based on focusing on coping, then on succeeding and then not having to longer suffer. Sara focused on processing painful feelings experienced when she was going through financial hardship, whilst paying her student's fee, preparing for several job interviews, and keeping multiple jobs at the same time. Sara developed a temper and became more energetic, dynamic, and brilliant in her achievement, albeit interpersonally sensitive and offensive; this was also a Pattern that Sara displayed throughout the first leg of treatment.

A year later, Sara learned to identify emotions linked to dysfunctional interpretation in interpersonal relationships, so she could then distance herself from unhelpful patterns of behaviour, linked to her past personal story. Sara was able to respond interpersonally based on what she valued, i.e. help other people and be a good partner.

At the end of therapy, Sara reflected that what really matters is what she does on a daily basis, and this was what she needed to be happy. Sara is now a Deputy Commissioner and continues to be in a relationship with her partner.

References

Beck, A.T., Kovacs, M., & Weissman, A. (1979). Assessment of suicidal intention: The scale for suicide ideation. *Journal of Consulting and Clinical Psychology*, *47*(2), 343–352.

Boniwell, I. (2016). *Positive psychology: Theory, research and applications*. Oxford: McGraw-Hill.

Dahl, J., Plumb, J.C., Stewart, I., & Lundgren, T. (2009). *The art and science of valuing in psychotherapy. Helping clients discover, explore, and commit to valued action using acceptance and commitment therapy*. Oakland, CA: New Harbinger.

Dell'Erba, G.L., Frascella, M., Leo, M., Mascellino, R., & Mariano, E. (2020). *Resilienza*. Firenze: Aldenia.

Dell'Erba, G.L., & Nuzzo, E. (2010). *Psicologia Pratica*. Lecce: Pensa Editore.

Ellis, A. (1994). *Reason and emotion in psychotherapy* (2nd ed.). New York, NY: Lyle Stuart.

Hadot, P. (2000). (contributor) *Manuale di Epitteto*. Torino: Einaudi.

Legrenzi, P. (2019). *Storia della psicologia* (6th ed.). Bologna: Il Mulino.

Robertson, D. (2019). *The philosophy of cognitive-behavioural therapy (CBT)*. London: Taylor and Francis.

Seligman, M.E.P. (2018) *The hope circuit*. New York: Perseus Book LLC.

Warburton, N. (2007). *Philosophy: The basics*. London: Routledge.

Chapter 7

Acceptance in Psychotherapy

7.1 General Aspects

Acceptance brought together different cultures and left evidence of this in religious texts, such as Sutra, Bhagavad Gita, the New Testament, and Tao Te Ching; in several philosophers Nietzsche, Kierkegaard, etc., and also in several literary works written by Shakespeare, Nabokov, Austen, etc.

Acceptance is from the Latin *accepere*, and it means to receive and to prepare to receive. There are four main kinds of Acceptance:

*   Acceptance of events as they are, and of our own limitations
*   Acceptance of ourselves, with a focus on personal value as human beings
*   Acceptance as opposed to stigma and prejudice
*   Acceptance of stimuli, without attaching judgement

Acceptance has become relevant to personal growth and psychotherapy. Acceptance as a factor is in fact implied within certain conceptualisations of psychological problems (Woods & Kanter, 2007).

*   Depression and grief
*   Interpersonal conflicts
*   Panic disorder
*   Obsessive-Compulsive Disorder (OCD)
*   Neurodegenerative disease
*   Adjustment disorders

Furthermore, resilience and Acceptance are similar constructs, as they are both based on the appraisal of frustration.

DOI: 10.4324/9781003299226-8

7.2 Acceptance and Meaningful Life

As discussed in a previous publication (Dell'Erba & Nuzzo, 2010), accepting an event not only means to establish the legitimacy of receiving that event but also implies a decision that establishes what may be experienced and accepted.

Acceptance does not mean to resign to our fate and to adopt a pessimistic stance, and suffering due to loss. It is beyond this. Throughout Acceptance, a person has already overcome loss and has genuinely accepted distress associated with frustration.

To accept something means finding reasons and clarifications. It is not possible to accept something without building a model that can explain it, or reasons that can justify it (Dell'Erba & Nuzzo, 2010; Miceli & Castelfranchi, 2014). As already mentioned, there are two different levels of Acceptance:

• To accept a specific problem or event
• Acceptance of our limitations and ongoing self-awareness in this regard

In epistemology, Popper discussed a problem and devised a solution (Severino, 2004). To exit the trap of confirming a hypothesis, he indicated that a hypothesis may be falsified, as an explanatory suggestion to describe and understand scientific revolutions and the advancement of science. Popper suggested conceptualising theories as conjectures, and their progression as an attempt to refute them.

A theory can explain Nature's phenomena and understand how to make sense of experiences. If we think about this knowledge as conjectures, then it is valid until these concepts are refuted, which makes them falsifiable and therefore not utilisable. Advance through refuting and falsifying attempts means to further the application of a schema of knowledge to test its validity, and therefore its usefulness. Our memory stores the acquisition of knowledge and how we learn.

Theories, but also human behaviour, may act inflexibly, in autopilot mode, and may be excessively driven by biases and schemas. There is a further process that counteracts schemas, and experiences, keeping in mind experiences in the present moment; it is the other side of furthering our knowledge which supports psychological functioning at its core.

Acceptance is to keep in mind that frustration stems from expectations. The dynamic processes between these constructs, schemas, and experiences date back to philosophical differences between Plato and Aristotle to then move to Kant, who focused on devising a solution between empiricism and rationalism. Knowledge, experience, and goals as basic processes of behaviour and human psychology represent key aspects to comprehend Acceptance as a pillar of psychotherapy (Woods & Kanter, 2007).

Acceptance is knowledge of the state and is concerned with updates on conditions posed by reality. It gives meaning to life and how to dedicate our life to authentic goals.

7.3 Practice Acceptance

The ubiquity of Acceptance within a vast number of contexts and psychological problems has given us the opportunity to explore its typical amplitude in a referential meaningful way.

- Justify other people's views or the situation that caused damage, whilst comprehending a different perspective from ours, which is legitimate and independent from our own
- The damage we suffered may be repaired, whilst comprehending and focusing on what matters to us and what is within our power, whilst validating impersonal aspects of frustration, as part of lived experiences rather than personalising or ruminating on human badness, and getting lost in the attempt to determine the motivation of others
- Evaluation of frustration experiences depends on whether there are alternative perspectives and if our experience can be addressed from a practical perspective within our power
- Comprehend adversities in depth and forgive, accepting our vulnerabilities as human beings
- Find things to learn throughout adversities, reframing and finding opportunities in difficult circumstances
- Make the most of a negative situation. We can reframe a difficult situation, so we may obtain the best realistic scenario within a context. This scenario is often conceptualised as a way of being tested, thus continuing to focus on practising flexibility towards optimum functioning and contentedness
- Reappraise the evaluation of frustration of an adversity and its consequences by considering it in the context of a wider, challenging scenario. This results in a realistic appraisal, which incorporates our limitations and Acceptance of the laws of Nature, or God, for those who believe in religion
- Consider a loss or adversity as an extra not initially considered; this is linked to Kahneman's theory of subjective perspective of rationality (Kahneman, 2011)
- Decide to not engage with the Zeigarnik effect (as previously discussed, it postulates that people tend to recall unfinished or unresolved tasks, rather than completed and solved problems). Thus not link a loss or damage to a series of losses but accept each event, in line with the general perspective to accept our limitations as human beings

- Be autonomous and evaluate when required as to whether it is realistic to rely on other contexts or sources of information. This results in reframing or to renounce our expectations and simply focus on what is within our power. Recognise what is authentic and meaningful and focus on our resources
- Feeling supported by others along with affection and understanding helps to distance ourselves from loss and to live within our possibilities, whilst accepting our limitations and respecting the laws of Nature. This means not to wish what is not within our power, accepting that this is for the greater good; in this context, Acceptance is facilitated by our ability to clearly argue the context of the matter
- Accept help available if needed and rely on someone's support, thus accepting to relinquish power and ability to do so to others. When this has an authentic meaning, it is facilitated by others' support and knowing that there is help when we need it the most

7.4 Acceptance as Synthesis of Psychological Input

Acceptance is a complex process; however, it may be summarised in psychological interventions (Hayes & Hofmann, 2018) that define its components. We attempt to outline those components as follows.

An initial component is to redirect ourselves towards accepting that we are human beings, and as such part of Nature, and not as individuals gifted with powers and special features that exempt us to function as the rest of Nature does. This is a realistic stance and allows us to share our being with what surrounds us. This aspect serves as a motivation, in that it is forgetting this context that leads us to ask for help from someone, who may then deal with consequences stemming from this, or lack of boundaries. We can consider this as "being on track," growing, developing, and being part of a greater order.

As previously considered, to accept an event it is important to accept existence and our lives as they are; this is the Stoic Path formulated by Seneca, Epictetus, and Marcus Aurelius (Robertson, 2019).

A further aspect is to accept experiences as an integral part of leaving full and meaningful lives, without resistance or avoidance. To live means to expose ourselves and realistically translate subjective representations of practical problems (Dell'Erba, Frascella, Leo, Mascellino, & Mariano, 2020).

Emotions in these contexts are an integral part of being human, not problems to cure and solve, perhaps with some astute trick; we would define this as the Existential Path, as in Heidegger and Sartre (Warburton, 2007).

A third aspect is to have and to knowingly possess a perspective, meaning that we are aware of how we perceive our mind, both in its content and its functioning. Being unable to recognise such content, resist thoughts, or compensate (and fall into traps, as a fish with a bait hook) is part of the problem. The other part is to evaluate mental states as problems and act against them, by sabotaging normal processing, or cognitive functioning. We would define this as the Cognitive Path (Robertson, 2019).

A further aspect is represented by integration. When I live my life meaningfully, I accept my living as part of several experiences, which are integral parts of our living; we would define this as the Flexibility Path (Hayes, Strosahal, & Wilson, 2013).

We feel that Acceptance incorporates all of these psychological processes. They are part of Integrated CBT, which is emerging from the clinical and theoretical psychotherapy field (Hayes & Hofmann, 2018).

7.5 Brief Thoughts on Acceptance

Acceptance is deeply connected to psychological pain and suffering. Frustration is what places us at the forefront of emotional suffering; this is directly proportionate to the importance attributed to the goal and to missed opportunities to circumvent frustration. Therefore, Acceptance in the context of compensatory strategies is considered unhelpful. However, the subtle balance between compensatory strategies and beliefs related to the goal under threat is not to be taken for granted. We accept significant losses, previously deemed extremely important, untouchable, and non-renounceable, as long we could protect core goals deemed non-negotiable (Young, Klosko, & Weishaar, 2003).

One of these goals is to maintain a reasonable realistic positive sense of self. Each challenge that poses a threat to our self-evaluation as loveable, efficient, worthy individuals is destined to be dealt with as an alien cell by our immune system.

Defences in relation to a threat are the beginning of the negotiation and appraisal of what can be relinquished or lost to maintain our beliefs inflexibly pursued.

7.6 Hurdles to Acceptance

What is important for us to accept? Information, self-evaluation, someone else's judgement, or evaluation? Each information that connotes the status of pursuit in progress or a threat posed to a crucial goal becomes the focus of attention, as it is strategic.

When information alerts us to a problem, we instinctively consider the fastest solution, which does not compromise the overall strategy, as it would have a significant emotional cost, given that it would require making new decisions for each frustration.

Psychological suffering is functional to the perception of compromised goals, as well as all of the compensatory strategies deployed to process such suffering. As long as there are opportunities to cope, we may not accept that frustration is orientated towards something important. Thus coping may lead to overconfidence, and tragic events led by our arrogance, with self-deception playing the main part in the maintenance of this process.

We are not forced to accept something, until we may operate and engage in maintenance work, in practice details. The more we believe we can correct and compensate, the less we are ready to accept what is important to us.

Hurdles to Acceptance are characterised as follows:

* Our own difficulty to discern that something should be accepted, especially what is out with our power and control. This is a point that might be misunderstood in several ways, thus becoming a barrier to realism, adaptation, and emotional well-being
* What is the focus of our attention, and what becomes a goal that we wish to achieve? For instance, if a person suffers, he is no longer able to achieve this goal, to the detriment of the cognitive effort required to reconsider his valued sense of direction. Thus this person's goal will morph into avoidance, in order not to suffer or not focus on redirecting his cognitive efforts and commitments. However, those goals are impossible to achieve. The consequence of all of this will be to inadvertently create new psychological problems and suffering caused by unachievable goals. A classic example is to remain trapped on secondary problems that become recursive and characterised by vicious circles. Avoiding experiencing anxiety, which might result in experiencing more anxiety or blaming ourselves due to feeling sad, might create more sadness and disappointment
* A further consideration is linked to biased arguments to justify frustration and Acceptance. For instance, as mentioned above, the argument of the "Laws of Nature" works only if we accept as individuals that we cannot change them. This is because to accept a limitation, it is necessary to accept that we have limitations

If the above considerations are not addressed, Acceptance will be obstructed.

7.7 Full Acceptance vs Prospective Acceptance

One of the ways to conceptualise Acceptance is to consider it as a way of devising our goals in keeping with facts, on what reality offers to us (Hadot, 1995).

A further way of conceptualising Acceptance is constructive, strategic, and subjective.

This is captured within the following scenario.

A patient who suffers from depression, and the loss of her father, but blames herself due to the selfishness of her suffering, which is so overwhelming that results in neglecting other relationships, including her young son, and suffering even more to observe her own suffering and feeling worse compared to how she felt when she was feeling better and able to control.

In this instance, multiple factors are contributing to the worsening of the situation, with significant rigidity and inflexibility; with an impoverished and superficial perspective of herself as a human being. Furthermore, from a psychological perspective, there is nothing that may offer a reason to accept what is out of our power, such as the loss of an elderly, sick person.

Experiencing the loss of a loved one seems unsustainable if perceived as an inconceivable disgrace, to which is added suffering for not being understood by others. It is the lack of adherence to the fact that this is out of her control that destabilises her and keeps her stuck in her psychological suffering.

Comfort stems from comprehending that there are events out of our control and that focus on short-term relief, almost "deluding myself that I can keep my father alive," originated avoidance strategies, regarding processing the loss and short-term relief of grief.

For other individuals, psychological suffering is characterised by their inability to comprehend how to accept frustration stemming from the lack of achievement of certain goals, i.e. reputation, negative judgement, and anticipatory anxiety. In these instances, understanding ourselves as human beings with our limitations means to admit and therefore accept that we face unpleasant, painful experiences, which are also part of a bigger picture that we cannot anticipate or foresee.

Focusing on the Laws of Nature or God's Will does not always result in justifying such perspectives.

We are horrified and shocked when considering the injustice suffered by entire populations. These events, far from being justified as an inevitable fate due to nature or divine will, were, after multiple attempts, subverted. Increasing our power to make our wishes come true or values of respect, freedom, contrast in certain people what is happening. Acceptance is always at a higher level; it requires, however, substantiation in a specific context; otherwise, it will morph into passive submission and fatalism.

What is considered external and considered a "divine intervention" may be quickly dismissed as external to what is within our power due to the subjective representation of our individual skills, as human beings (Hadot, 1995). What was external to our control is now internal or can be internal within a different context.

If a condition is automatically external, its Acceptance does not affect our goal to be fulfilled and achieve what is important to us, even if meaningful action is symbolic and suggestive of an ethical drive within our existence.

Action and Acceptance are contextualised in an ethical and moral framework when whatever is meaningful is not pursued. It is not unheard of that suffering is linked to the absence of ethical conscience, concerning what is good and what is evil to ourselves and to others.

7.8 Acceptance and Self-Deception

How much awareness do we have regarding the Acceptance of reality? How much pressure is the goal to adhere to reality even when we experience frustration and loss and emotional pain?

Trying to perceive and discern what is true can result in a detachment from reality, thus learning information about the environment that surrounds us; this is essential for survival.

Adhering to reality, which is an internal, subjective aim, is incongruous with the desire not to suffer, which in the long-term and in non-emergency situations is integrated with the goal of being well.

This function remains focused on survival, through obtaining information from the environment and through avoidance of pain (which signals a physical problem). Objective individual aims can be directed towards short-term avoidance of suffering, deferring the reminder of the problems.

There is, however, a further function at work, especially in complex organisms: knowledge (De Houwer, Barnes-Holmes, & Barnes-Holmes, 2018).

Knowledge's coherence, although imperfect, is a requirement for timely adaptation. The lack of Acceptance towards reality and information, whilst addressing the avoidance of pain in the short term, undermines in the long-term building the foundation of sufficiently coherent knowledge. This is usually the price of self-deception. A person avoids what makes him suffer, but he collapses in chaos produced by a lack of knowledge and struggles within an inflexible conflictual dynamic.

The ability to accept conflict within our mind as a normal occurrence allows us not to create new psychological problems and self-perpetuating traps. Endurance and Acceptance of a reasonable inner concept, and reasonable mistrust in our compelling wishes, lead to good maintenance of our psychological well-being.

The antidote to the dangers of self-deception is a combination of humility and privacy.

Accepting what is happening in the here and now seems to indicate that we cannot rely on anything, focus, and start over from the here and now (Hayes et al., 2013). However, we cannot escape memory, what we learned in the past, and knowledge as a compass and understand our own environment.

The ability to keep in mind what we learned and specific content from our minds enhances individuals' ability to balance what they know with what they desire in a given environment. This adds further psychological individual abilities, consisting of reminding himself that he has a mind and is not subjected to a passive and deterministic relationship with his own context. An individual knows that he can choose and by choosing he accepts the facts and affirms his actions.

7.9 Case Example

Maxim is a 29-year-old man, who lives with his parents. He has a diagnosis of Schizophrenia and receives benefits due to this condition. Maxim receives treatment from a Community Mental Health Team and is supported within a work placement project.

Maxim had a two-year history of emergency admissions to a psychiatric unit, and he was subsequently admitted to a psychiatric hospital.

He was referred to one of the authors for psychological input.

Maxim had two main therapeutic goals:

- A safe place where to explore his difficulties and worries
- Learn to understand his mental states and related emotions through psychoeducation

Maxim responded to treatment, and once he overcame sedation and family difficulties by receiving additional psychological input with his family (his parents and a younger brother), Maxim started to work on auditory hallucinations and delusions based on beliefs of supernatural and persecutory nature.

Psychological input supported normalisation and conceptualisation of auditory hallucinations, by using visual tools in the clinical room.

Maxim's input was subsequently focused on challenging other features of auditory hallucinations, i.e. content, influence, and impact on his functioning.

All of these factors were explored and reviewed every time Maxim reflected on his experience of hallucinations.

Psychological treatment gathered increased momentum when Maxim kept a diary of voices, which led to conceptualising psychotic-driven interpretation as alarmed and excessive, as part of the therapeutic work in the session.

Maxim developed an increased ability to distance himself from such hallucinatory episodes and to understand the antecedents of challenging events that occurred during the week.

During a particularly challenging session, Maxim disclosed sexual abuse perpetrated by a family friend and neighbour when he was seven years old: an episode he never disclosed to his family. Maxim also disclosed that he misused amphetamines and cocaine for 3 years (from 16 to 18 years old), when he was in secondary school, along with methylenedioxymethamphetamine (MDMA, ecstasy in tablet form), the latter misused when Maxim went to the disco club.

This led to the identification of high-risk symptoms, perceptual disorder, visual hallucinations, persistent doubt, irritability, and impulsivity, which were dated back at least 4 years before the onset of Maxim's psychotic symptoms. Such experience was conceptualised collaboratively with Maxim by normalising some aspects of his personal history, whilst attempting to formulate his symptomatic responses as emergency reactions, whilst taking into account the cognitive distortions caused by drug misuse.

This resulted in contextualising predisposing factors and vulnerability to dopaminergic medications, which he fully understood. This surprised Maxim's parents in the process, as his parents were confused by his personal boundaries and overinvolvement at the beginning of the process.

After 8 months, Maxim was able to identify situations that could generate stress, including relational and family stress. He is not presenting with hallucinations and has distanced himself from doubts concerning persecutory and supernatural phenomena.

Maxim continues to receive psychological input for psychosis, which is now much more focused on interpersonal problems and job placement; his response to treatment has been good, along with an improvement in general functioning.

References

De Houwer, J., Barnes-Holmes, D., & Barnes-Holmes, Y. (2018) What is cognition? A functional-cognitive perspective. In S.C. Hayes & S.G. Hofmann (Eds.), *Process based CBT*. Oakland, CA: New Harbinger.

Dell'Erba, G.L., Frascella, M., Leo, M., Mascellino, R., & Mariano, E. (2020). *Resilienza*. Firenze: Aldenia.

Dell'Erba, G.L., & Nuzzo, E. (2010). *Psicologia Pratica*. Lecce: Pensa Editore.

Hadot, P. (1995). *Philosophy as a way of life: Spiritual exercises from socrates to foucault* (with J. Carlier and A.I. Davidson). Oxford, UK: Blackwell.

Hayes, S.C., & Hofmann, S.G. (2018). *Process based CBT*. Oakland, CA: Content Press/New Harbinger.

Hayes, S.C., Strosahal, K.D., & Wilson, K.G. (2013). *Acceptance and commitment therapy*. New York, NY: Guilford Press.

Kahneman, D. (2011). *Thinking, fast and slow*. New York, NY: Farrar, Straus and Giroux.

Miceli, M., & Castelfranchi, C. (2014). *Expectancy & emotions*. Oxford: Oxford University Press.

Robertson, D. (2019). *The philosophy of cognitive-behavioural therapy (CBT)*. London: Taylor and Francis.

Severino, E. (2004). *La filosofia contemporanea*. Milano: Rizzoli.

Warburton, N. (2007). *Philosophy: The basics*. London: Routledge.

Woods, D.W., & Kanter, J.W. (Eds.). (2007). *Understanding behavior disorders: A contemporary behavioral perspective*. Reno, NV: Context Press.

Young, J., Klosko, J.S., & Weishaar, M.E. (2003). *Schema therapy. A practitioner's guide*. New York, NY: Guilford Press.

Conclusions

In this last section of the book, the core aspects of the cognitive foundation, starting from the ABC model, will be discussed and summarised. This is a schema whereby

- A is the activating event, or stimulus of an individual's focus
- B represents the evaluations and interpretation and thus the meaning that an individual gives to A
- C is the emotional state and the emotional and behavioural responses stemming from the evaluations

Opting for the ABC model facilitates considerations relevant to psychological functioning. This option leads to conceptualisation of psychological problems, in a way we feel is clinically efficient, whilst theoretically convincing.

Emotional Problems Are the Consequences of Individuals' Interpretation

ABC's model establishes that "C" are consequences. The feelings that we experience, such as anxiety, depression, stress, irritability, guilt, and shame, are emotional responses that may be identified as C, as consequences of our evaluations and our judgements that we might formulate in relation to antecedents (A).

This is an underpinning prerequisite of contemporary psychology, which despite its several conceptualisations places activities such as appraisal representation and evaluation at the core of our behaviours and our psychological life. In practice, it places the reasons for our behaviours amongst our psychological life.

Appraisals or evaluations rely on what is most important to a person, what are the most important aims or intentions; some are shared and widespread, and others are more subjective and personal.

DOI: 10.4324/9781003299226-9

Most importantly, motivation represents the fulcrum of a person's actions, whilst bearing in mind his knowledge and experiential foundations, which shape his specific perspective.

Our behavioural and emotional responses are likely to be coherent with emotional states, only because of such cognitive structures such as inferences, judgements, and evaluations. This might facilitate ongoing appraisal of outcomes based on an individual's main goals and intent.

All emotional states may be defined as C and can be schematised in a specific category, which is the one pertinent to consequences, reactions, or responses, and may be of emotional or behavioural nature.

Emotional Problems Are Determined by Evaluations

ABC's model asserts that psychological problems and thus emotional states are regulated by behaviours and not by life events, facts, and circumstances as intended. Behaviours determine consequences.

In other words, an individual's emotional problems are influenced by evaluations, judgements, inferences, and hypotheses, and most certainly not by events or occurrences per se, or by descriptive events.

We focus our attention on Bs being concerned with what is relevant to the individual, his scopes, his boundaries, and values. Moreover, what is appreciated is not just the ultimate accomplishment, but also intermediate goals, which are required to achieve or that represent a threat.

For example, a man is left by his partner and becomes depressed. What caused depression in this context? Is it caused by his partner, or his own appraisal of the situation?

The answer is that the individual's appraisals and judgments are the precipitating factors that lead to experiencing depressed feelings.

Specifically, the individual will have experienced a negative appraisal of loss concerning his own future opportunities to repair this relationship, and probably a self-critical belief of himself and his own resources, directly or indirectly, blaming himself for experiencing that feeling, thus determining a recursive secondary problem.

A further example is represented by an individual who experiences irritation and anger in the context of conflict with their manager. What are the factors that activated such powerful emotion? Was it the manager who behaved rudely and abruptly, or in an aggressive and invalidating manner instead? Is it therefore the event in itself, or the antecedent within the A-B-C model? Or is it the particular evaluation and appraisal of the individual that determines whether someone has the right to behave in a certain way or not? Or what a person may and may not do that might lead to anger, and in particular to an evaluation based on Tort (unfair damage)? This person might think that their manager does not have the right to treat them in such a way, therefore activating anger, through the evaluation of the event of suffering injustice.

Thus, as considered so far, individuals are not emotionally activated by facts, events, and stimuli, but by their own personal appraisals, cognitive processes, and evaluations, that might concern themselves, or life in general. All these beliefs are concerned with the monitoring and pursuit of our ultimate goals, whether they are conscious or not.

There Are Links between Specific Evaluations and Specific Emotions

Another implication of the ABC model is that there are preferential and prioritised links between our evaluations and appraisals on what occurs and our emotional responses.

There are some strong links between evaluations and cognitions concerning important goals and objectives, and our emotional state. For instance, in the example mentioned above, the appraisal in terms of injustice, namely the person who thinks that they are suffering unjustly, is linked to emotions of anger, irritation, and hate.

Appraisals linked to loss, like thoughts on losing a loved person, low self-esteem, loss of friendships or power, or an important relationship, social status, or reputation, are emotional states linked to sadness.

When a pessimistic appraisal, characterised by hopelessness, is added to sadness, a person's emotional state will be depressed, rather than just characterised by sadness.

We experience fear and anxiety when we estimate an increased likelihood that a threat will occur. In a similar fashion, we experience anger when we fear that our public image or reputation will be damaged. In the latter case, we might also experience shame and embarrassment.

Cs are the categories concerning emotional reactions and responses structured around core emotions such as joy, sadness, fear, anger, disgust, and astonishment. These are bio-behavioural structures, phylogenetically predisposed, and are universal responses shared with our fellow human beings, on every part of the planet, regardless of culture and education.

Humans, unlike primates, are more developed socially and have more complex mental states, and therefore raw core emotions are rarely experienced as such. Nevertheless humans are enriched by evaluations, thoughts, reasoning, and planning; in their subjective form, this process generates emotions as complex states such as feelings, which are the most peculiar trait of our psychological (inner) life, pride, melancholy, embarrassment, guilt, and contempt.

Our Appraisals Originate from Our Personal History

A corollary of ABCs of human behaviour within a trans-theoretical inte-grative framework is that certain meaningful thoughts, evaluations, and behaviours are related to the way in which we developed and learned core important information about ourselves, who we are, how we think, on how we think our parents have brought us up, their guidance, and on the expecta-tions towards ourselves and others. Attachment, care, learning experiences, and memories concerning significant relationships originate a general sub-jective model, which has the purpose to provide us with foundations so that we can orient ourselves, process information, and focus on our goals.

B's foundations are rules, beliefs, and general information and may be considered answers to our personal theories and assumptions regarding our life history. According to contemporary psychology (Legrenzi, 2019), these personal ideas may be conceptualised as schematic structures or schemas, i.e. core beliefs that we keep within ourselves from a very young age, as they somehow have been part of a foundation of other more specific beliefs linked to specific aspects of our lives (Alford & Beck, 1997; Beck, Freeman, & Davis, 2004; Dell'Erba, 1993, 1998; Guidano, 1988).

For instance, a girl asks to be accompanied, as she has established a pat-tern of dependent behaviours, which are linked to her fear of being alone and being unwell when on her own. This hypothesis may be linked to a deep rooted belief of vulnerability or consider herself at risk of develop-ing an illness. Those behaviours may also be a consequence of early life experiences, whereby she may have learned directly or indirectly through observation, that her health is poor, and therefore she is at risk and has to be shielded. This example illustrates some core beliefs, at the core of our mental states, that stem from individuals' history.

A key factor is the person's belief to have suffered damage in the past and still be affected by it. This is simply a mental state which occurs in the present, a cognition that the individual thinks now, thus experiencing the consequences in terms of emotional activation currently, even if the content of this thought is linked to past events.

This is not an explanation of how the past influences the present, but explains how a person's beliefs, which are current, thought and believed in the here and now, activate certain emotional states.

Similarly, the same situation would occur if a person were evaluated to be predisposed to certain negative situations and catastrophic circumstances, particularly damaging to his future.

In this case, his emotional state is not caused by the future, but by what in each moment in the present the individual thinks about the future, future which is, of course, unknown, even if some individuals take these hypothe-ses for granted.

B determines C, and B is determined by the individual's history.

Change in Evaluation Modifies Mental States

An ulterior implication of ABC is reflected on the therapeutic work required to change thoughts and evaluations, i.e. interventions that aim at modifying certain unhelpful assumptions or hypotheses; the work on B effectively changes emotional, affective states and their behavioural consequences.

This is because a person may reconsider how certain aims and goals are compromised, threatened, or irreplaceable, how and to what extent recalibrate strategies and goals, without excluding a re-evaluation of what is important, and how to keep focusing on what is meaningful to him.

Let us consider loss, for instance.

• When processing loss, we might believe we are responsible, for such an event rather than the contrary
• We might consider loss as the beginning of other incumbent losses, rather than considering it an isolated event
• We might conceptualise loss as being longstanding, rather than transient, thus leading to the maintenance of sadness, which will keep this process immovable and self-perpetuating

Psychotherapy intervention not only encourages to re-evaluate Bs (re-evaluate what matters) to modify C (emotional states), but also any discussion or exchange of ideas influences re-appraisal; in fact, is this not the way in which we console our friends?

Interventions on Bs, which facilitate C, may be conceptualised as any other intervention that acts on the portrayal of our own goals and on the outcomes of their pursuit, that is the belief that certain goals may or may not be threatened.

Every therapeutic intervention, even if psychoeducational in nature, should incorporate that psychological interventions of any nature may promote, reinforce, clarify, or reassure those certain individual goals, whether broad or more focused, that are possible, and some means to pursue them are more realistic and beneficial than others.

A Psychological Problem Can Be Conceptualised through an ABC Model

A problematic concern ought to be conceptualised by an ABC model, by considering the key aspect of the problem as perceived antecedents and "events under focus," cognitions, and consequences.

A problematic event may be conceptualised by more than one ABC, hence by more than one mental state.

Several ABCs can be serial or parallel processes, depending as to whether one may trigger the other (or the others) or that a unique event stimulus is evaluated in Bs in several and simultaneous ways, thus originating simultaneous consequences, resulting in mixed, alternating, complex emotional states.

A C of anger, after an evaluation of an unfair event, may represent the stimulus, for instance, through the operationalisation of selective attention of physiological sensations, for an evaluation of the self as at risk, sick, or in danger (as evaluation of secondary B), thus activating panic and anxiety (in secondary C). Interpretation of physical sensations as A often originates alarm-focused, vicious anxiety circles, which are the main features of anxiety disorders (Beck, 1976; Beck & Emery, 1985; Mancini, 2005; Miceli & Castelfranchi, 2012; Wells, 1997).

ABC model affords conceptualisation of the problem in a pragmatic manner, so that pertinent interventions may be devised collaboratively, whilst being understandable and approachable by the person who is experiencing the problem.

CBT's ABC affords several clear-cut differences and operates fine-tuning of psychological mental states, which seem of essence for constructive, functional, and adaptive processing of the events, whether positive or negative, in such a way that maintains a focus relevant to the individual.

A series of differences and abilities derives directly and indirectly by the utilisation of ABC, and by the psychological analysis of an individual's mental states, concerning the events that are related to the goals that the individual has set.

CBT's anchorage to the ABC model taps into a vast methodological inheritance of therapeutic structure, and a plethora of techniques orientated to change in perspective and therefore of action in relation to what is meaningful to the individual.

This book based on CBT as foundation for psychotherapeutic integration could be interpreted as a panacea for assimilative integration. We argue that there are not acceptable reasons to disregard an approach that has produced the best clinical outcomes, effortlessly accessible and falsifiable, based on future data and mental processes in general psychology. This approach offers, in our view, an optimal solution in the field, currently.

In the chapter on integration, we attempted to draw attention to the need of clinicians for the development of integrative models in practice, which on one side are effective, whilst not losing their wealth and breadth of suggestions derived from other approaches, and solutions that we considered suitable for integration.

One of the main challenges outlined is the vast choice of proposals and languages in psychological practice, which are not always consistent with clinical psychology practice at a professional level.

In this context, it is critical to encourage and deliver the dissemination of evidence-based psychotherapy outcomes and clinical psychology based on good clinical standards.

Some processes and contents considered requisites of psychological formulation were utilised as a field to integrate different approaches, which merge seamlessly with our approach within this project.

Not only ABC but the dialogue between aspects of the self, mental processes, our own, and others' metacognitive knowledge, evaluations, functional and dysfunctional coping, and in conclusion emotions and their functions. All these aspects have proved how CBT can be integrated without imposing Procrustean tolls.

The third chapter stressed how several cognitive factors may contribute to clarify, within a contemporary psychology key, several psychological problems on the basis of the understanding of cognitive processes of social and general psychology, in such a way to include entanglements and dilemmas of human behaviour and psychopathology, always within a clinical psychology practice perspective, i.e. paradoxes and psychological traps, interpersonal challenges within the therapeutic relationship.

The interpretation of the clinical-theoretical perspective is to validate "normal" psychological processes and to conceptualise and comprehend psychological problems and suffering with interpretative tools provided by contemporary general and social psychology.

A key to understanding this clinical theoretical perspective is to appreciate "normal" psychological processes and to conceptualise psychological problems and suffering, as interpretative tools of contemporary social and general psychology.

The fourth chapter contents explored some of the main features of our advanced CBT approach, focusing on the complexity of some recursive, self-perpetuating psychological problems. Secondary problems, the correlative challenge of accessing consciousness in the first person, and mental states, for instance. All of these are examples of an advanced integrative approach "contaminated" by valid theoretical and technical ideas, but in an explanatory framework quintessential to a strengthened and validated CBT.

The fifth chapter focused on training and the challenges posed within and by psychotherapy pedagogy and teaching. One of the transversal themes identified was related to the core competencies informed by learning clinical psychology interventions and methodology based on practice. We raised concerns in this context and encouraged personal development as part of standard training, whilst acknowledging several logistic and organisational challenges.

The sixth chapter outlined the attempt to incorporate structures tangential to psychotherapy within a wider perspective; such structures (constructs) are traditionally introduced in a context pertinent to social and positive psychology.

We argued that hope, acceptance, and resilience comprise the fundamental aspects of evaluation and regulation of our goals, and as such part of the foundation structures that best explain human suffering.

The seventh chapter provides greater coverage of acceptance's psychological processes in a wider and more strategic context. We propose that such processes underpin individuals' motivational and regulation processes, and not only in relation to the vast and fertile philosophical contribution previously discussed.

Struggles in acceptance provide a valid explanation of subjective individual suffering, whilst processes that are supportive and facilitate acceptance, of what is not or is no longer within our control, are one of the most significant leverages in psychotherapy.

A Few Words about the Authors

Dr Clara Calia obtained a PhD in Psychology at Queen Margaret University in Edinburgh (2016) and a Clinical Doctorate in Cognitive Behavioural Therapy in Italy (2014). She also completed a PgCert in Academic Practice at the University of Edinburgh (2020) and in Cognitive Neuroscience at Oxford Brookes University (2010), as well as an MSc in Clinical Psychology (2008).

She is currently working as a senior lecturer in clinical psychology on the Clinical Doctorate in psychology at the University of Edinburgh (UK) and as a member of the anti-racism group in the Clinical Doctorate in the UK and the Human Rights Consultant group of the British Psychology Society (BPS). Clara also worked as the Ethics & Integrity Lead role in clinical psychology and, between 2019 and 2022, as Deputy Director of Research (Research Ethics and Research Integrity) at the School of Health in Social Science at the University of Edinburgh.

Social justice is the main drive of her research and clinical work, by promoting principles of equity, ethics, participation, and dialogue with culturally diverse populations and those at risk of social injustice.

Dr GianLuigi Dell'Erba is a clinical psychologist currently working in the public health services, in mental health settings. He pursued specialist training in CBT for Psychosis and Advanced Statistics and continued to further his knowledge and training in CBT, Short Dynamic Psychotherapy, and Clinical Criminology. He subsequently became a lecturer and CBT supervisor. Dr Dell'Erba wrote eight books and co-authored over 80 articles; he is also interested in the psychological profession and positive psychology. His general interests are focused on philosophical and psychological aspects of living well, subjective satisfaction, and well-being. He always remains, in an active way, a lover of knowledge, music, good food, and the good individual and relationships.

Dr Ernesto Nuzzo carries out his activity as a clinical psychologist in the Health Service of the Puglia Region (ASL Lecce) and is the author of numerous publications and three books on clinical psychology and psychotherapy.

He is a lecturer in CBT in the Clinical Doctorate APC in Italy. He worked for a few years as a psychologist, clinical criminologist, and technical consultant for the Civil Court. Recently he became a clinical manager at psychiatric rehabilitation facilities in Italy.

Ernesto Nuzzo likes to define himself: man, living person, and stoic.

Donatella Tamborrini is a senior psychotherapist trained and accredited in Cognitive Behavioural Psychotherapy, Interpersonal Psychotherapy, and Family-Based Treatment for Anorexia Nervosa. She is a certified FBT supervisor and an adjunct member of Professor Lock's Training Institute of Child and Adolescent Eating Disorders at the University of Stanford.

Donatella provided child and adolescent CBT supervision at the University of Edinburgh from 2012 until 2022. She currently works for the NHS as a senior supervisor and in the private mental health sector. Donatella obtained an MSc in Cognitive Behavioural Psychotherapy at the University of Dundee in 2010.

Donatella is an EEATS Scholar; her clinical focus is devoted to treating young people who suffer from severe anorexia nervosa, eating disorders and mood and anxiety disorders, whilst supporting their families. Donatella's focus throughout her career has been on delivering the highest quality of care for her patients and clients, and teaching to her students.

References

Alford, B.A., & Beck, A.T. (1997). *The integrative power of cognitive therapy*. New York, NY: Guilford Press.

Beck, A.T. (1976). *Cognitive therapy and the emotional disorders*. Madison, CT: International Universities Press.

Beck, A.T., & Emery, G. (1985). *Anxiety and phobias*. New York, NY: Basic Book.

Beck, A.T., Freeman, A., & Davis, D.D. (2004). *Cognitive therapy of personality disorders*. (2nd ed.). New York, NY: Guilford Press.

Castelfranchi, C. (2012). *Goals, the true center of cognition*. In F. Paglieri, L. Tummolini, R. Falcone, & M. Miceli (Eds.), *The goals of cognition*. London: College Publications.

Dell'Erba, G.L. (1993). La dinamica della AutoImmagine: Uno studio sulla valutazione di sè. *Psychopathologia, XI*(5).

Dell'Erba, G.L. (1998). *La Psicologia del Pensiero nelle Scienze Cognitive*. Rassegna Studi e Ricerche. Istituto di Psicologia Università di Lecce, Lecce.

Guidano, V.F. (1988). *La Complessità del Sé*. Torino: Bollati Boringheri.

Legrenzi, P. (2019). *Storia della psicologia* (6th ed.). Bologna: Il Mulino.

Mancini, F. (2005). L'egodistonia. In B. Bara (Ed.), *Manuale di psicoterapia cognitiva*. Torino: Bollati Boringhieri.

Miceli, M., & Castelfranchi, C. (2012). Sofferenza Psichica. In C. Castelfranchi, F. Mancini, M. Miceli, C. Castelfranchi, F. Mancini, & M. Miceli (Eds.), (a cura di) *Fondamenti di Cognitivismo Clinico*. Torino: Bollati Boringheri.

Wells, A. (1997). *Cognitive therapy of anxiety disorders: A practice manual and conceptual guide*. Chichester: Wiley.

Index